Thank God I'm an Agnostic

THE CHOIR PRESS

Thank God I'm an Agnostic

Trusting Your Hunch about God,
the Universe and All That

Art Lester

First published in the United Kingdom in 2025 by

The Choir Press

ISBN 978-1-78963-547-8

I would like to extend my thanks to Steven Appleby for designing the cover artwork

Agnostic: a person who holds the view that any ultimate reality (such as God) is unknown and probably unknowable

Dedication: To the Quartet

And thanks are past due to Steven Appleby, for all his help making my books look more interesting than they are. Also to Charles Miller, who weighed through much of the book's material while it was still a brewing idea. Special thanks to congregations in London, Paris and Dublin for keeping me honest.

Chapters

Foreword

Agnostic.

This word, like almost every English word that is difficult or confusing, comes from the Greek: *a* (without) and *gnosis* (knowledge). If you are an agnostic, you are among the millions of us who think the truth about God, the Universe and all that is basically unknowable.

Agnostics come in several varieties. Some worry about the God thing all the time and keep trying to find a religion that makes sense. This may be futile, as the very name suggests. Another type of agnostic is the most common. These are the people who basically never give the whole thing a thought.

Look down the list below and see which of these statements most closely resembles your ideas:

1) I'm pretty sure God must exist. I mean, look at the flowers and stars and all that. I just don't practice any religion.
   You are a theist.

2) God probably exists, but he's not in contact with human beings. He built the Universe, probably, but then left it to run on its own.
   You are a deist.

3) There is a God, but He's not really in full control, which is why there is bad stuff in the world. Forces of evil fight against His will.
   You are either a dualist, a Manichean heretic or, possibly a Zoroastrian.

4) There are lots of Gods and spirits in a great cosmic dance.
   You are either a Hindu, an animist or a New Ager.

5) Everything is God. It is another name for nature or the Universe.
   You are a pantheist. That means this book is God, too.

6) Yes, everything is God. But he created it all and survives both in and beyond it, immanent and transcendent.
   You are a panentheist.

7) There is no God; He cannot exist.
   You are an atheist. You have no business here on page 5.

8) God? I haven't got a clue.

Congratulations! This book was written for you.

I can seem a little harsh with what I call "mere" atheists in the pages that follow. That isn't because I'm any more intolerant about religion than I am about everything else. It's more the result of simple observation. Atheism is unlike agnosticism, in that it reaches a conclusion, a final statement of fact. In that, it is the first cousin of uncritical fundamentalism. *Certainty* is its most important feature. It is impatient with unanswered and unanswerable questions.

Religions have always hated the idea of uncertainty. That is what has made them strong. The whole idea is to get the facts about God, the universe and all that, set them down in creeds and doctrines, and then find a way to enforce them. In the early days of Christianity, there were so many different ideas around that the newly formed church in Rome had to keep holding big councils. In what is called the Chalcedonian Creed, written in 451, the matter of being confused was dealt with, once and for all:

... one and the same Christ, Son, Lord, only begotten, recognized in two natures, without confusion, without change, without division, without separation ...

So much for any lingering doubts. There was to be no room at all for confusion.

No one hates not knowing stuff as much as an atheist. But what about all those born-again believers? Well, we religious freethinkers have always found a way to denounce nonsense, and I don't think the time to stop is now. Not now, when the world, suffering from an overdose of rapid change, is polarising fast. But the trick will be to denounce the empty, fear-ridden pronouncements that spring from a too-literal belief without condemning the poor souls stuck in that all-too-appealing trap.

For me the best way is to own the fact that not only do I not know the truth about everything, I don't think the human mind is capable of understanding it, any more than a dog can look at the spots on a page and see that it is the written word. The best way is to learn to feel comfortable, even happy, in not knowing, and to communicate that happiness as much as the Bible-thumpers convey their shaky edifice of belief. Not to avoid confusion, but to embrace it. I think that might be holy. I think we could call that "holy confusion". It merits a special place for the second most beautiful three-word phrase in the language: "I don't know."

If you're someone who feels that they have got the answers, you've read too far already. Best to put the book back on the shelf, or – better yet – to give it to someone who is grappling with finding the right questions, let alone answers. The rest of us will carry on looking for the blessings that can only be found in uncertainty.

Sundown in Eden

It's late afternoon somewhere in the Fertile Crescent a long time ago.

God's six days of hard work creating everything is over, and after a day off, He puts Adam and his newly created partner, Eve, in a position of power over birds, fish and animals. They are instructed to fill the Earth and "rule over it". All the plants and trees in the world are theirs to exploit at will, except for a tree planted in the centre of the Garden of Eden – the Tree of the Knowledge of Good and Evil. But given the richness available in this paradise, that shouldn't be a problem. It seems that the only two people on the planet are now in complete control.

Or are they?

Despite God's best intentions, a random element turns up to ruin the plan. This is the Serpent, whom the Book of Genesis describes as "more crafty than any of the wild animals God had made." Some theologians say that this is another name for Satan, the Tempter. Others have made this reptile responsible for all human vice – especially sex.

The Serpent targets Eve for his project. This is either because she is weak (male chauvinist interpretation), or because she is gifted with more openness and is a better listener than men (feminist view). Whatever the motive, Eve apparently likes the idea of eating the fruit of the forbidden tree, which the snake says will "open her eyes" and make her wise, like God. Not only that, the Bible says it tastes good. She offers a bite to Adam, and his eyes get opened, too.

The first insight they get is that they're naked. Panicked, they stitch together some fig leaves and make some sort of loincloth. Just then, toward sundown, they hear God approaching and dive into the shrubbery to hide.

In the first two chapters of the Bible, God is portrayed as a vast presence beyond His creation. But in this tale, He takes a stroll through Eden in the "cool of the evening", which seems to indicate that He, like humans, dislikes the heat. Strangely lacking in omniscience, He calls out, 'Where are you?'

Adam and Eve have been rumbled. When asked to explain why they are hiding, Adam blurts out, 'We were ashamed because we were naked.' This prompts the first big theological question in the Bible: Who told you that you were naked? The story tumbles out: the Serpent is to blame. And Adam, grassing up his spouse, blames Eve for suggesting that he break the rules. And he's blamed her ever since, it seems.

God's verdict is swift. They are to be exiled from Eden. To ensure that they can't creep back in, there will be a permanent guard of cherubim on duty, as well as a flaming sword, set to move back and forth like a pendulum across the entrance.

But that's not all. He sentences the Serpent to a life of crawling on his belly and enmity with women, so that he can be crushed under human heels. Eve is condemned to painful childbirth. For good measure, He tacks on that she will only be able to fancy her husband and that he will rule over her.

Adam's punishment is to leave behind the easy pickings of the garden and to start to work in agriculture, where the sweat of his brow will often produce only thistles and weeds. And there is loss of immortality, when God says, 'You came from dust, and to dust you will return.'

This story has appeared in various forms in the traditions of many cultures. The descent from contentment in an innocent state of unknowing, followed by exile into a life of uncertainty and discomfort has been the subject of lament for thousands of years. It is often called "the fall".

It does sound like a fall. But is it? Or did the Serpent do us a favour?

Adam and Eve are now homeless, condemned to scratch a living from the Earth and to experience pain and death. Grim as it may sound, they get away with something that God apparently never intended: human intelligence.

Because Eve dared to taste the fruit that, once and for all, made her aware of the duality that comes with human intelligence: good v evil, light v dark, life v death; she became something like a modern human being. Adam, despite being a slow learner, went along too.

So, looked at from a different angle, it seems more like a blessing. This banishment from the happy non-awareness of the beast is the beginning of virtually everything that we cherish: imagination, ingenuity, intelligence, logic, art and science. The curse or blessing of self-awareness brings with it the knowledge of one's own death, but it also gives rise to genius.

Exile from happy unconsciousness brings with it another element: doubt. When they passed through the Eastern Gate of Eden, they carried with them the ability to wonder and to disbelieve.

Which is where most of us reading this book come in.

Hunch Theology

Browsing through Facebook one day – in between having sublime and profound thoughts, of course – I saw a notification from a guy I used to know well. He is in his late thirties, a talented artist with a growing list of admirers, the father of two beautiful kids and with a lovely Spanish wife.

Here is what he said: 'What is the meaning of life? That's easy: nothing. There is no meaning to life. You are here because your mum and dad wanted children, or at least they wanted sex. There is no higher, deeper meaning to existence.' He went on to say that you should try to enjoy it, and, if possible, make it better for others.

I don't know why I found that shocking. A lot of my friends would self-identify as atheists, and I'd be lying if I didn't admit to having had atheistic thoughts myself over the years. I think it must have been the dismissive tone you so often hear with statements like that. Almost as if he means to say, 'Ha ha! Everything you might believe in is absurd and pointless.'

There are good, thoughtful people in plenty who disbelieve in any sort of God, and their ideas are not only welcome, but often seductive. But I don't know many who are prepared to trash the idea of meaning in any form. Even the hard-boiled genius Jean-Paul Sartre, father of modern existentialism, was able to cook up a concept of what he called "good faith" as a way of encountering the universe.

When you come out of a state of anxiety and confusion about the ultimate meaning of everything, it feels great. For the fundamentalist, it is the experience of being born again. They are enviable in one respect: everything they need is contained in one volume of two testaments. The Christian ones share this with the Muslims – everything you need to know is right there, chapter and verse. Never mind if the book was the result of political wrangling and infighting and has been edited to express the values of succeeding figures of power. You can overlook the bits where a presumably loving God suggests stoning gay people and exiling people who wear mixed fabrics. You can read it the way a child watches Dr Who

– from behind the sofa. It is important to overlook inconsistencies, cruelties and nonsense, because what is at stake is that wonderful feeling of certainty, of knowing all there is to know about everything. Or at least knowing that everything can be known.

For the "new" atheist, things are similar. Each new quark and black hole discovered or indicated on a computer screen brings fresh proof of the accidental workings of the universe. Each trait newly attributed to genes brings a fresh dose of certainty, like a drip feed of painkillers. They are looking for a gland in the brain called the "God spot", which will explain away, once and for all, why the belief in a divine being is universal among human cultures. Down with God and all that; long live certainty.

In a following wind, you can forgive both these positions. Uncertainty is uncomfortable. When certainty begins to slip away, we feel lost and desperate. That's why we cling so long to outmoded cultural norms, and why it is natural to resist change. That's one reason why the pandemic is so terrifying. If you have always been held fast by a culture, a network of family and society, and things happen which threaten to erode that security, you feel powerless and confused.

The forces let loose by the insights of physicists and mathematicians, let alone the new technology, have begun to erode the stable foundations of the world as we have always known it. There is a "paradigm shift" under way, and we are all a bit baffled. We can hardly hope to keep up with technology, and the days before Facebook have been lost. It is no wonder, then, that we will grab at any form of certainty when it comes along. In 1930s Germany, the Nazis offered a new myth and leader, but what they really offered was a route out of the confusion that followed defeat in WWI. Things are not so very different now, and it is already possible to imagine a new messiah or idea that would grip all but the wariest among us.

Living without certainty is a hard path. The Unitarian statement about "living in the questions" hardly scratches the surface. Forming a new theology, making a new formula to live by seems impossible in the stream of change we are all swimming in.

So how exactly do we live in uncertainty? If we are to avoid taking the first exit into a tightly fitting new strait jacket, how are we to manage it?

Here's what I would say to that most poignant of human questions. We can get by only through a single human trait. This trait is one we all share. The new-born infant cries at birth. You can see this – I do – as a prayer. Why would you cry if you didn't somehow sense there was someone there to hear you? What would be the purpose, even in the opinion of a committed Darwinist, of such a thing?

Of course, you might scoff at this. Say it is an alarm mechanism wired into us, a biological response to ensure care for a vulnerable creature. You can also say that a beautiful sunset is merely dust particles refracting sunlight. Or that a baby's smile when he first sees you is merely an evolutionary ploy to make himself too cute to leave on a hillside. You can say these things, but – go on, admit it – they don't feel right somehow. That points to the fine edge of our enduring mystery. And the only means we have to penetrate it is what I would call a hunch. A hunch which is the tip of a great iceberg of meaning shared, in its depths, by all of us.

I think we are all born sharing one thing. That thing is the capacity for trust. Trust that, whatever your degree of ignorance and helplessness, you are somehow held in a net of meaning that transcends theories and questions. It is a wired-in quality of us human beings. Justified or not, explained by some evolutionary cause or other, the question hangs there: why would we think that?

And yes, that leaves us where we started. Certainty simply isn't available right now, as we wend our ways through the twists and turns of life. But maybe we have a compensation. A deep-down sense that, whatever we discover – or do not – we are not lost. Call that faith if you wish. I call it a hunch.

My own hunch is reinforced by something quite simple. It was best expressed by the late Dr June Bell, a Unitarian from Edinburgh. At a conference one day, after some exhausting exercises in making and un-making theology, she came up with this:

'I'm from here,' she said. 'It's my home. So I think everything must be all right.'

Seeing Air

I've got a Somalian friend who is a minicab driver. His name is Jesus.

No, that's not his real name. He got it by accident when he was told he needed to put his Christian name on a form, not just his surname. Jesus was the only Christian name he could think of at the time. The nickname stuck.

Jesus is a Muslim. We have odd theological conversations while he drives me home once a week. He's not devout; he's a Muslim because, if you're born in Somalia, that's what you are. One night we were talking about British people, and Jesus said, 'They're all Christian.' He was laying down a marker: if they're white and born here, they're Christians. I said, 'You're forgetting that a lot of them are other things, like Buddhists, Jews and atheists.'

'What is an atheist?' Jesus asked.

I realised that, in his mind, I had just spoken nonsense, and the more I explained, the more complicated it seemed to get. He couldn't grasp the concept that anyone could not just not believe in God, but believe in NO God. So he just clucked his tongue and I shut up.

Then, one Thursday evening, I was talking to a man who came to see a film in my church. He expressed some curiosity about Unitarianism. I was explaining that, because we have no creedal statements, we have people with a wide variety of beliefs. Christians, yes, of the very liberal variety. Religious humanists, the odd Buddhist, a few Muslims, maybe even a Jedi knight or two.

'But I'm an atheist,' the guy said, in that way I have heard so many times. Said as if it is still a radical position, and not the default setting of millions in the UK. It always makes me sigh. 'You have everything but atheists,' he went on. I had to gently correct him. I said, 'Oh no. We have lots of atheists, and agnostics, too, and sometimes everyone in the room is an atheist, at least for that day. Including me, the preacher.'

Things have reached a point where the question, "Do you believe in God?" isn't really even asked any more. It's just assumed that no one does outside a small loony class and some diehard Anglicans, all over 80.

Why is that? Put simply, it's because the idea of God just isn't logical. You can't prove it. You can't build a giant Hadron collider and capture a photo of a guy with a white beard. You can't even identify where He might live, even if He did exist. It's not logical, it's not scientific, so it's not true.

Jesus of Nazareth was a standing source of illogic to his friends. You can read between the lines of stories like that of Mark, and see that, whatever you thought of him, you were doomed to be in a more or less perpetual state of amazement if you followed him around. I'm not talking here about the miracles; there has been too much water under the bridge to get a grasp on what really happened. Those famous events will have suffered centuries of well-meaning alteration by the faithful. I'm talking about those things which have slipped through the net of official history, by which it is possible to get an impression of the man unedited by theory and faction.

To start with, he often seemed to talk in riddles. Parables, yes, but it appears in ordinary speech as well. When his mother came to find him during the early part of his ministry, imploring him, as a good Jewish mother should, to give up this mad mendicant act and settle down with a nice local girl, he said, 'Who is my mother?' Asked why his disciples, including the owner of a local boozer and a supposed prostitute, had no religious practice like the strict rules of John the Baptist, he said, 'Why would you fast when you are with the bridegroom?' Not only that, he would disappear into the woods or the desert every once in a while, leaving his followers confused. He would get mad at a tree and zap it, smile and be sweet to the crowds of secret agents trying to trip him up, work on the Sabbath, allow his feet to be washed with precious oils when money was tight, and even have a chat with a Samaritan widow – about the lowest creature there was in those days.

His economic theory was just as bad: the two annas of a widow were worth more than a bull calf in the temple. Inexplicably enraged outside a *bureau de change,* he spilled shekels all over the shop. Finally, given a chance to escape from certain death, he waited mildly in an olive grove for the soldiers. Trying to understand Jesus was like trying to see air.

Now I think it's time for a disclaimer. Lately, with the rise of what is called the "alt-right", logic and reason have come under attack. Experts, or people who actually know things, are routinely dismissed. Not just by Bible Belt loonies, but by cabinet ministers. The latest entry in the OED one year was "post truth".

So am I doing the same thing, when I speak of a logic – and a reality – we can't yet see or understand? Well, no. I'm claiming the opposite. Where the "post-truth" crowd want you to believe something unreasonable, like global warming being a Chinese hoax, I'm asking us to do what Alfred North Whitehead called the greatest intellectual achievement of the 20th century: suspend judgement. Instead of filling our minds with absurdities, I'm asking us to keep them open, to watch for new truths as they emerge.

That's because it seems that there may be something we aren't able to see, but which has its own logic. Realising this, we have got two choices. One, dismiss what these voices have been telling us through the centuries, cobble together some pale logic like, well, that was then; we know a lot more these days. Or, two, let the riddle do its work on us. Let it be cause for second thoughts as we pass our days getting and spending, make us more ready to stop and watch the next time we pass somebody talking in what seems to be riddles.

Am I insisting that God does exist, despite logical evidence to the contrary? Well, no. Before I made any such assertion, I would have to ask you to define your terms. What do you mean when you say "God"? Are you speaking of the Old Man of the Sistine Chapel ceiling or some more mystical notion, having to do with spirit? Do you mean it like a metaphor, or as a statement of scientific fact?

No, that's not what I'm doing. What I am doing is introducing the notion that if there is one thing that can be demonstrated, over and over again, it is that we don't know what it is that we don't know. If we're unable to conceive of things like the parallel universes scientists keep turning up – I think there are currently four, by the way, or is it seven? – how would we recognise them when they bump into us relying on textbook physics?

One way I like to think of it is to imagine a dog, a Labrador Retriever, say, looking at a poster on a church board. Next to her is a woman, her owner, also looking at the poster. The dog sees a green object made of metal and glass. And a white area covered in spots. Not very interesting, except perhaps as something to sniff for doggy messages. The woman is reading the words "Service 11 am". Both are seeing, but the human, being of a different degree of awareness, is interpreting. If the retriever could think about it, she would think her owner was mad to be staring at the spots. Behaving illogically.

History has taught us that in each succeeding generation, things are brought into awareness that simply weren't there before. Within recent times, outside of a few old Greeks, nobody much had ever heard of an atom, but within a blink in cosmic time, we were busily splitting them and creating a fearsome amount of energy, seemingly from nothing. Until they began to unravel the mystery of the human genome, nobody understood why brown-eyed people could have blue-eyed babies.

Maybe people like Jesus of Nazareth and the other great souls weren't being quite as illogical as they seemed. Maybe the illogic was ours. Being the equivalent of a Labrador Retriever, maybe we just didn't know what it was we were looking at.

I do understand how avowed atheists get to where they are. Despite some evidence to the contrary, I rely on logic myself. And when those apparently meaningless things we are all prey to surface from time to time, I can look up at the starry sky and see – not the home of God, but a vast, swirling, unfeeling cluster of gases and cold rocks. A cluster which doesn't care and isn't capable of caring about little me. In those times, the very idea of God seems like a cruelly debunked fairy tale.

But then something prompts me, and I think, *What do you know?* I hear voices from the past, saying, "Electricity is all smoke and mirrors." And "Man will never fly," and I tell myself: What you don't know is far more thrilling and enormous than what you do. You may think of yourself as a fearless pioneer of the truth, but you really have more in common with the advocates of the flat earth theory. When you define the future in terms of the present, you always will get it wrong. You see, you don't know yet what it is you don't know.

Down there underneath the smarty-pants ideas I rely on, something prods me. Maybe it's the so-called "God gland" scientists have been looking for without success. Something wired into my nature that all the logic in the world can't quite make to shut up. I call it a hunch, like the hunch of detectives in novels. Or like so-called feminine intuition. Or like the faint hunch of scientists before they discover something that was there all along, but invisible to the unquestioning eye. You can call it faith, if you must. The author of the book of Hebrews, 1600 years ago, called it "The substance of things hoped for, the evidence of things unseen."

I prefer to realise that virtually everything I know is something I didn't know before. A few years ago, it seems, I was bemused by what they were calling the "information superhighway". The term "Internet" hadn't yet soaked into my brain. Now my life revolves around the Web and all sorts of digital technology. I wasn't stupid then; I was just unaware.

The next time someone asks me if there's a God, I won't get defensive. I won't waste time saying, well yes there is, but please don't confuse me with the fundamentalists, or the Pope. I'll say something like this: 'I don't know yet, but I have reason to believe – good reason to believe – that someday I will.'

Someday we all will.

Welcome to the Real World

Just as soon as I'm elected King of the World, there's a phrase I'm going to declare illegal.

This is a phrase you've heard a lot of times. It's said as a kind of put down, a marker that you're somehow smarter, more clued up and sophisticated than other people. You look at someone and say, in a dismissive tone, 'Welcome to the real world.'

What this usually means is that the object of the comment is a fuzzy-headed dreamer, not really savvy enough to understand how things really work. It has synonyms: "Welcome to Planet Earth" is one. Another that's gaining ground comes from a TV advert: "Wake up and smell the coffee." I've had it said to me, more than once. It means something like this: your ideas are not much more than fantasy. Grow up. Things just don't work that way.

I've found that this line of talking is usually employed by those who want to justify The Way Things Are, and who want to do that because they in some way benefit from it. We hear it now in the condescending tones of people who say that good economic policy involves making things easy for billionaires so that some of the pixie dust of entrepreneurship will rub off on us scruffy millions. "Welcome to the real world." We hear it in the croaking voice of Gordon Gekko, the "greed is good" guy from the Oliver Stone film. "Welcome to the real world." We hear it in the justifications for our support for dictators, both now and in the past. "Welcome to the real world." Is someone praying that their cash-strapped lower division football team can somehow beat an oil sheik's hobby club in the Champions League? "Welcome to the real world."

But what is this "real world" they're talking about? If I had to analyse it, I'd say that it is a world of hopelessly stacked odds, which you ignore at your peril. That being the case, you learn how to play the system, and dismiss idealism, optimism and faith as childish and useless indulgences. This world is composed of hard edges and is solely materialistic in its outlook. And, because that's the case, fuzzy-headed notions of cooperation replacing raw competitive behaviour, for example, are not just unrealistic, but downright silly. Fairy tales. What matters is something known as "the bottom line".

This way of looking at life isn't new. In fact, you might think of it as the default position of humanity. It's the same mentality that wants to relegate poets to irrelevance, whip children out of their dreamy world and exile and execute prophets. Take Socrates, for instance.

The Athens of 400 BC was an up-and-coming society. They had invented a form of democracy, though that was limited to property-owning men. They had Olympian gods in place, though even then people didn't pay all that much attention to religion. Socrates was a bit out of place. He often refused to wear shoes, for one thing. He was ugly, with an outsized head, and didn't wash all that much. He was popular with a gang of young people who thought he was cool. He taught them things *al fresco,* in an olive grove and sometimes in bars. He had a different take on "the real world".

We don't have a single word actually written by Socrates. Most of what we know of him comes from his disciple, Plato. It was he that developed the philosophical school called Platonism, a form of which is still around. In basic terms, Plato believed that the world we see – that which can be weighed, described and measured – was a pale reflection or shadow of the real world. His most famous exposition of this idea came in the Parable of the Cave.

He asked pupils to imagine a cave, completely cut off from sunlight, in which men (it was always men, I'm afraid) were chained in place with their heads pointed toward a wall onto which the shadows of puppets were projected. Kind of an early cinema, maybe, or a nascent form of virtual reality. Because they didn't know any better, they believed that what they saw on the screen was reality. Then, Plato said, imagine one man who is able to slip his chains and make his way to the cave entrance. He walks blinking into the sunlight, and for the first time sees things as they really are. It is so overwhelming that he can't take in what he is seeing. He only knows that what is before his eyes is real, and that the images on the cave wall are not.

There's no happy ending to the tale, though. When he goes back into the gloom and tries to tell others what he has seen, they at first think he is mad, then subversive. Finally, they have no choice but to kill him. That's what happened to the subversive Socrates, by the way. The senate declared him to be dangerous to the young minds he was teaching, and he was required to drink a bowl of hemlock tea; poison, to us.

The central meaning of Platonism is that we only imagine that what we see is real, when it is actually just a pale version of a much more significant reality that lies outside our ability to perceive. The way to access this reality, or leave the cave, was through philosophy – though we can interpret that today as religious experience as well as mere reason. "Welcome to the real world" meant transcending the poor version of truth we're accustomed to and finding a higher one.

Most people, Socrates said, were – get ready for some Greek here – *"eu a moussoi"*, literally, "content without the muses". In other words, happy to live a flat, materialistic life, ignoring the hunches and intuitions of something finer and more real.

You may think that the senate was right to silence Socrates. After all, he was telling young people, or showing them how to discover, actually, that the so-called "real world" of the time wasn't the whole picture at all. Radical stuff. Stuff that threatens to rob power from the establishment. One way he did this was by declaring that beauty and truth were one and the same. That what we call beauty is a beckoning intuition toward the *really* real. But if you take the side of the senate, you might be surprised to discover that the farther we advance in philosophy and even fields like quantum mechanics, the more reasonable Plato and Socrates seem.

The philosophical rage of the past few decades has been postmodernism, in which ideas were "deconstructed", or analysed outside their context. We now know that everything we know, or think we know, is filtered through a screen of relativity. Heisenberg told us that the very act of observing something changes its nature. Anthropologists like Margaret Mead altered the societies they were trying to study. Light is both a wave and a particle, depending on which scientist you're talking to. We now realise that knowledge itself is a dodgy proposition; two people observing the same thing see differently – sometimes radically so. Old absolutes have been evaporating like dew drops on a car bonnet. The slogan of the Beat Generation said it like this: "Compared to what, man?"

The tendency to enforce the establishment view of the real world sounds like the crude images inside Plato's cave. Shadows on the wall. The view from our cave is less reliable the more we find out. Is this the "real world" the cynics want us to live in? When Socrates invited his pupils to live in the real world, he meant something else.

Up against the real world, Socrates thought of where we spend our time as the world of materialism. Now, that word has been hijacked to mean a kind of eager consumerism, maybe someone who is miserable without 200 pairs of shoes. It does reflect the real meaning of the word but doesn't do it justice. Materialism is a way of looking at reality that says that everything, absolutely *everything* that is, is composed of matter and energy. That includes consciousness, by the way. So materialism, the world of Plato's cave, is all about stuff. If you can't put a ruler to it, plunk it on a scale and measure it, register its velocity, etc., then it simply doesn't exist.

Virtually all of current science is enmeshed in this idea, and that's reasonable. It was never designed to reveal the meaning of things; only to say how they work. From a completely materialistic perspective, Plato's real world cannot exist; if it did, we would have discovered it, maybe in the Large Hadron Collider. That's it then. The guy who escaped from the cave was having a hallucination. If he kept on about it, you'd have no choice but to kill him, would you?

Well, out that particular window went poetry, art and mystical experience. There went love, too, inasmuch as they will one day discover an enzyme under a microscope that explains it away. There went the gasp of breath that happens when you see a mountain sunrise that makes you want to drop to your knees. And there went the moment of recognition – yes, recognition – that you experience on first viewing your new-born child.

But wait, you silly denizens of the fantasy world. All is not lost. A lovely guy called Stephen Jay Gould published a paper in 1997 that offers a way round this problem. His idea is called "non-overlapping magisteria". Yes, that is a mouthful. But here's what he means by it: that both scientific materialism and spiritual experience are true. They each have what he called "teaching authority", but there's one problem: at no point do they overlap. That means the big project is to determine the boundaries.

Right now, the scientific, materialistic side is making most of the running. The "real world" of the materialist is in top form, and the quiet little intuitions of the religious are having a rough time. That makes the sneers of the *"eu a moussoi"* possible. As Socrates said, they're quite happy to live without the muses and to ignore the deep intuitions that animate those of us who feel that there must be something we've overlooked or not learned yet to see.

But it's more than just a simple difference of opinion, you know. Decisions that affect people's lives are being made from that materialistic vantage point. It's right to wonder whose lives will be made miserable by adhering to their so-called "real world". Families in Aleppo? African farmers who share a river delta with a big oil company? Old people whose pensions have been halved by austerity programmes to please the world's investors? You can make your own list.

When I first heard of Plato's notion of a realer world that lies just out of sight, I seemed to understand what he meant. Nothing I could put my finger on – just what I'd have to call a hunch. Every once in a while I have a moment's intuition that seems to tell me that there is more, much more, to what I call my life than I am able to comprehend. I would hate to have to prove it, but then, I don't have to. I'll leave all that to the scientists.

But what I'd really like to do is take charge of that phrase and say to everyone, 'Welcome to the real world.' The really real world that we can only dimly make out from here, but that something un-measurable, un-weighable and with no registered velocity at all tells us is where we're headed.

And maybe, someday, where we belong.

The Invasion of the Book Believers

Do you know how sometimes very small, apparently insignificant incidents stay in your memory? One such for me was a few years ago, when I was coming out of a Tube station in South London. A young man was blocking my path. He fixed me with steely eyes, and as I approached, I could see that he had business with me. Or at least he thought he did.

'Are you saved, brother?' he wanted to know. He was clutching a Bible with what appeared to be white knuckles.

I admit that I was at a temporary loss for words. And those who know me can imagine how rare that is. I began to mumble something, I can't remember what now. What I remember is those piercing eyes of his, and the way he was clutching the clearly well-used Bible like a drowning man clutches a rope thrown down a well.

A few years ago, I saw some similar eyes while watching a television report of the 7/7 London bombings. They were the eyes of Mohammed Sadiq Khan, a teaching assistant from Beeston, Leeds, in a posthumous video justifying his part in the slaughter of innocents. Bright, insolent in their certainty, the eyes said it all: here was a man who had moved from the bleakness of ordinary human confusion into the promised land of divine assurance. I never saw the eyes of the 9/11 suicide pilots, and I have never seen the face of a man who has pressed the detonator of a bomb in an American abortion clinic, but I'm sure they all shone with that same gleam of holy certainty.

I have come to think that the white knuckles of the man clutching the Bible looked that way because he was holding what was, to him, a lifeline. It was a lifeline because he thought of himself as drowning. But drowning in what?

For an answer to that question, we have to go back a century and a half, to a time when a bright but reportedly difficult young man stepped back onto English shores from the decks of a small ship called the *Beagle*. He was carrying a lot of burdens: years of samples of exotic flora and fauna from a long voyage that took him to the remote places of the known world. Notebooks too heavy to carry, boxes of papers that would stagger an archivist. But he had one burden that was invisible to the eye, and that one was even heavier. He carried his newly found evidence that the Bible stories were fictional, and that creation was the result of explainable natural phenomena instead of a six-day mega-miracle by the God of the Old Testament.

It took Charles Darwin nearly two decades to publish his results. He knew that his book, *The Origin of Species,* would not just set the scientific establishment alight with speculation; he was aware that theology was also about to change forever. If it had not been for a possible competitor for scientific glory, it is possible that Darwin would have chosen to publish his work posthumously. He didn't have to worry about money, after all; his uncle was Josiah Wedgwood, and his family were secure enough to offer him the life of a gentleman as long as he wished. But I also believe that his theory was sort of radioactive, and that it simply had to be revealed.

It would be lovely to report that the world had recovered from these revelations and gone on finding a way to trust the universe without keeping the bath water alongside the baby. But you know, as I do, that the issue still divides communities and families, especially in America. And that those who are willing to shut down their logic to save God are growing like mushrooms. And so that was what the young man outside the Tube station wanted to rescue me from: a world with no God, no ultimate meaning, and – worst of all – no Bible. What he was inviting me to do was put my mind to sleep, ignore the evidence of my senses and my insight, and just *believe* the unbelievable.

I couldn't do that. And even though I don't know you, I'd be willing to bet that you can't either. But for some reason, it appears that we are managing to avoid the literal sinking feeling that motivates the True Believer.

Alongside these unhappy fundamentalists, we have recently been treated to a wave of what I have to call "mere atheism". You know who I mean. Richard Dawkins with his undoubtedly brilliant scientific mind asking and then dismissing all the wrong questions. Christopher Hitchins, never willing to miss an opportunity to shock and offend, taking the mickey, as the British say, out of the loony religionists and misrepresenting even the staid theological porridge of worthy Anglicans. *The God Delusion* and *God is not Good* were destined to be best-sellers before either man wrote a single line. Atheism hasn't had such entertaining advocates for a long time. It has produced a whole new group of book believers.

The problem with their position for me is two-fold. First, it strikes me as a bit – forgive me – adolescent. One of the great things about being an adolescent is that suddenly you know all about everything. You know more about things than your parents, your teachers, and certainly than those old greybeards of the holy books.

The first "out" atheist I ever met was in the ninth grade. His name was David P and he reportedly had the highest IQ in the school. He also was a victim of what looked like terminal acne, although I don't necessarily relate the two things One day in the school cafeteria, David stood on the table we were sharing, the result of a dare, and shouted, 'There is no God! If there's a God, let him strike me dead!' Instantly, without thinking, the rest of us fled from the table. Just in case. No one actually said so, but we were all thinking about lightning bolts, and I wasn't wearing rubber-soled shoes. As it turned out, David P got nothing more for his blasphemy than three days' detention.

The other reason why the seductive logic of atheism doesn't work for me is one of simple observation. Atheism is unlike agnosticism, in that it reaches a conclusion, a final statement of fact. In that, it is the first cousin of the brainless fundamentalism I mentioned earlier. Certainty is its lure and its *modus operandi.* But throughout my own experience, my understanding of things has changed over time, sometimes radically. What I knew when I was younger has given way to what I know now, either by modification or outright replacement. What that has done is make me wary of any final theory or claim to knowledge. It has made me believe that belief itself is an illusion, also subject to the shifting sands of relativity, not a rock, graven with absolutes.

That's why I am so fond of those words by the Indian spiritual master, Meher Baba: "Trying to understand God is like trying to see with your ears". It's a perfectly human, all too understandable mistake, but I have come to believe that the mind is excellent for such things as making traffic laws and working crosswords, but, when it comes to finding meaning ... well, sorry, but it's just the wrong organ. That sort of search, as the mystics have long reminded us, is best undertaken by the heart.

I'm assuming that there are no hard-bitten, confirmed atheists of the Dawkins variety who have managed to read this far. I'm also ready to assume that there are no born-again book believers in the house. I suspect that most of us are somewhere in the middle, sometimes perhaps wandering toward one end of the spectrum, sometimes toward the other.

But that makes it sound a little ... I don't know ... *bland,* maybe. Maybe the right way isn't about being bland and non-offensive. Maybe we are doing ourselves a disservice by even referring to those two erroneous schools of thought. Maybe we should ignore all the shouting and posturing and just get on with being spiritual beings in a confusing world. And maybe we should just get rid, once and for all, of this matter of belief.

Belief is what condemns the extremists of both camps to irrelevance. In the end, it's about *experience.* If the mind and its fixation on ideas inevitably leads us in erroneous directions, what we have left is an experience. And that experience – I'm aware that some of you may not like this term – has been called the "practice of the presence of God".

Keeping that process alive is critical. And not just for us. We are doing it for the world, whether we know it or not. That world where people are drowning in relativity, lost in materialism, fearful of violence, bewildered by sexuality, vulnerable to poisonous nonsense from extremists and smart alecks. Now I'm no Christian, liberal or otherwise. I don't like the concept of sin any more than anyone, but I would say this: if there is a sin, it would be the waste of our precious opportunity to open a space for what is real and true.

Sometimes I think I'm not such a fast learner. It's taken me years to realise what the right response to the fanatic's question would have been. When he said, 'Are you saved?' I should have responded, 'Yes, Brother. I was always saved – from the minute I turned up here.'

Not Drowning, but Waving

There's a little story that seems always to be told to ministry students of every denomination. It's by that most prolific of writers: "Anon." It goes something like this:

Once there was a rocky, windy shore of a great ocean where ships often ran aground, with much loss of life and property. Because of shifting shoals and sandbars, all attempts at warning lights and changing information on nautical charts hadn't helped much at all. Ships continued to break up in the violent waters.

A group of people got together and had an idea. They would build a sturdy little lifeboat and take turns watching for shipwrecks. Then they would dare the waves because their own familiarity with the waters made it possible to navigate over the shoals even in extreme weather. And so they did. They put the lifeboat in a little shed, and over the next years saved many sailors who otherwise might have drowned.

The fame of the little lifeboat station spread far and wide. Soon they decided to enlarge the shed and use it for meetings. They took so much effort with this that rescues started to decline in number. Finally, their lifeboat was placed on an altar at one end of the meeting hall, where people decorated it with flowers and sang lifeboat songs. As this happened, many more sailors started to drown.

A small group of concerned members pointed out that the original purpose of the lifeboat was being ignored. Their protests fell upon deaf ears, and so, finally, they moved a way up the coast and built a new lifeboat, which they placed in a shed. But after a few years, the new lifeboat station suffered the same fate as the first, and its original purpose was forgotten.

From time to time a new concerned group would arise from within the station, and they in turn would build a new station until the same thing befell them. Today there are lots of lifeboat stations up and down that coast, but many people drown.

Now it doesn't take rocket science to unravel this little parable. The lifeboat stations are churches, and the story unpicks a certain tendency within denominations to stray a long way from their original purpose, to the corresponding cost of their missions. The lifeboat becomes, not an instrument of rescue, but a pretty metaphor, worthy of being adorned and adored, but not employed. The lifeboat's original shed becomes a great hall, just as the descendants of the little groups huddled in the catacombs built cathedrals. The medium has not only become the message, but in fact has replaced any sense of purpose. Meanwhile, the sea rages, and people continue to drown.

This parable is undeniably full of good advice for churches. The loss of purpose is as old as church itself. In Revelation, the book usually attributed to John the Gospel writer, churches are already being chastised for wandering from their missions. This is around the end of the first century A.D., but Paul's blistering letters to new Christian franchises, now having become Bible chapters, are even earlier – from about 56 A.D. So there is no time, we gather, when mission wasn't hijacked by mere formalism and sometimes even worse.

There are even some useful warnings in it for enlightened beings such as ourselves and, as far as it goes, it makes sense to indoctrinate a ministry student with its sentiments. But there is one major sticking point in the story for me: the problem, you see, is the sea. I suggest looking at it with the detachment of, say, an anthropologist, to see what it can tell us about our age. Maybe it will reveal why I feel discomfort with the "Little Lifeboat Station," and why I hope it won't occupy much of our future ministers' time.

It is clear that the writer was concerned with *salvation,* just as were the readers who have so cheerfully adopted it. The rescue of poor lost sailors from death in those violent waters can only refer to the salvation of people from the currents of the sinful world, and their eventual consignment to a terrible end. The grateful wretches are pulled from the sea into a place of safety; they abandon their sinful ways for the hallowed dry land. The sea is bad, the land is good. Before, they were drowning; now they are safe. The boat is the engine of salvation; the church is rescue.

In some ways this rings a bell. The liberal theologian Don Cupitt has said that life since Matthew Arnold's poem, "The Sea of Faith", had become "a heaving tide of relativity", though that might be a paraphrase. Old certainties are gone; new ones have not yet emerged. Floundering in post-modern confusion, we can't see the shore either before or behind us. In such straits, even we might be willing to snatch at apparent rescue, as so many fundamentalists, of whatever faith, seem to be doing. The deeps of confusion and relativity make even the shallowest of certainties attractive. Better to clamber into a leaky and outmoded boat, say some among us, than to drown in this unpredictable ocean.

When I was training for the ministry an eon or so ago, we were expected to attend the annual retreats of the ministerial fellowship. This was three days at a lovely retreat centre, in which you got to meet your future colleagues and engage in workshops designed to sharpen your ministerial skills. They were very informal affairs, with a lot of pub time, some rousing hymn-singing and even the odd dash of romantic intrigue – but that's another sermon.

In one workshop, ministers were discussing ways to come up with sermon ideas. I was feeling oddly uncomfortable. The more people talked about their ideas, about picking a notable figure, for example, and doing a potted biography of same, the less I liked it. You could take a favourite hymn, maybe, and go through it line by line, it was suggested. I muttered to a friend I was sitting next to something like, 'And there wouldn't be anyone left awake to take the offering.' Uh-oh! I was overheard – nailed. The leader asked me to explain. She was smiling like a python. Emboldened by several nights of pub worship, I thought, *what the hell,* and said, 'I think it shouldn't be so hard to come up with something to say every Sunday, given the state of people and the world.' I was implying that coming up with some time-filling anodyne noise was worse than saying nothing at all.

Ah, idealism! Even though I was no longer young, I was green, like an old penny. And I had had the temerity to pass implicit judgment on a roomful of good, earnest professionals. I was sunk, and I knew it. Plus, I richly deserved it; my mouth has very often landed me in the deepest waters. But the leader was intrigued. I realised years later that she was probably grateful to me for raising the temperature of what was turning out to be a fairly tepid session. She wrote on the board, "Given the state of people and the world they live in, it shouldn't be hard to think of something to say to them." What followed was a formative hour for me, as we all had the chance to talk about how people really were these days, about the confusion and depression and sense of loss and even terror that seemed to dog almost everybody.

I don't know how many of you have ever preached. I'll tell you about it: when you walk up those pulpit steps, you had better have something to say. I love to use the phrase, "preaching the soul" from my favourite, Ralph Waldo Emerson. I think he says that because, if the sermon is truthful, it is the soul that is both hearing and speaking. And what the soul wants to hear about is the real business of life and living. Not potted biographies, unless that becomes a vehicle for that task. Not mere entertaining jokes or humorous anecdotes, unless they really unravel a knot of the soul's meaning. And the soul has no patience with over-intellectualised argument or needlessly stretched metaphors. It strains forward, to hear from another soul in a time of apparent soullessness and relativism. In the presence of dishonesty of any kind, it goes soundly to sleep. Or worse, heads for the door.

Which brings me back to the little lifeboat station. What seems to stick in my craw is the idea that anybody can claim to know the route to the salvation of others. Especially if their problem is that they are bobbing about in a sea of sin, that what is needed is some form of reform or correction, an overthrow of their natures. As if any one person or group has got the answers. Any boat that is having an easy time of things these days, you might say, just isn't paying attention.

The sanctity and safety of the dry land to which the rescuers propose to carry you isn't all that great, either. Most people who have been "saved" in the metaphorical sense seem to spend all their time defending their newly found truths. Instead of resting more easily, they seem to be even more in need of continual reinforcement. Often that means convincing others, making them members of their lifeboat society. The truth must be filtered through a tight screen of ideas, a test of so-called faith, before being allowed into the mind. This turns out to be the price of all that "safety", and it's a high one.

So if we dismiss the idea of salvation, of being pulled safely onto dry land, where does that leave us? After all, we are no less at the mercy of the waves. We have left witches and evil spirits behind for denial and alcoholic spirits. Pharaoh has let us go, but our addictions haven't. Family isn't necessarily a refuge either; sometimes it is more like an emotional obstacle course. Serpents don't speak to us, but we are shocked to realise that sometimes two contradictory things can be true at the same time. In the words of The Jefferson Airplane, logic and proportion have vanished. Wouldn't it be nice, wouldn't it be *wonderful,* if there were a sturdy boat we could scramble aboard and just ride peacefully away?

Well, no, actually. Because what we would leave behind in Davy Jones' locker would be our own souls. Yes, our own confused collection of experiences, dreams and memories that make us *us.* And it may be – take my word for it – that there is a reason to be where we are. There's a reason to feel lost from time to time, to cope with realities that were once as certain as Arnold's Sea of Faith dissolving like ice in a furnace. To live the life of this time and to do it with courage and awareness and as much skill as we can.

If we *are* floundering in a sea of relativity, we are not doing it alone. But I think we are doing something much more important: I think in our slow ways, clinging to each other for support and advice, we are learning to swim. That's our response to the pitching seas. We have reason to believe – call it *faith,* if you want, a *hunch,* if you don't – that something is working in and through us that is better than a magical rescue from a lifeboat. The Sea of Faith has become the sea of consciousness. God bless us, I think we *are* learning to swim. Reversing the words of Stevi Smith, we are not drowning, but waving, after all.

Now I'll wave. You wave back, please. And keep on waving.

Religion? No Thanks

I've got a friend named Pete. He's someone I respect and like a lot. He's an animation film producer with a list of credits as long as your sleeve. I've known him for about ten years now. He learned early on what I do for a living but has hardly mentioned it in all the time I've known him.

One day the subject of my day job came up. He seemed a bit surprised. I didn't comment. He went on to say that he was impressed but also seemed amazed that someone like me could be involved in a religion. He was implying that I seemed a normal guy, not a wishful thinker or a fanatic. The question was unasked, but it was written all over his face.

'That's easy, Pete,' I told him. 'We're not a religion.'

I have a feeling that that just made it worse for him I'll try and take some time to explain more fully later. But just to check my own words, I went and did some research. Unimpeachable Wikipedia says:

> A **religion** is an organized collection of beliefs, cultural systems, and world views that relate humanity to an order of existence ... Many religions have narratives, symbols, and sacred histories that are intended to explain the meaning of life and/or to explain the origin of life or the Universe.

As anybody who has run into people like me will know, we don't pass out cosmic explanations. In fact, we endlessly repeat our mantra of "living in the questions". We get nibbles of enquiry and occasional visits from people who turn up hoping we can provide answers for the problem of living, but they usually don't stick around. Only those of us who feel comfortable knowing that they don't know do manage to make of our gatherings their spiritual home.

Next time I speak to Pete, I think I'm going to go even further. I think I'm going to say that religion is bad. Maybe even evil. Then I'll have to explain myself, so I might as well start with you.

If you look at the history of modern conflict, starting with the crusades, what you find is a clash of deeply imbedded religious ideas. Christians wanting to liberate the Holy Land from the Muslim occupiers. Jews wanting the same thing, and managing it – just about – in 1967, when they took Jerusalem. Sunni Muslims want to destroy the heresy that is Shia; Shiites want to do the same to them. The Protestant faction in Northern Ireland want to extinguish the heresy led by the Pope. Tamil separatists, who are Hindus, get massacred by the Sinhalese, who are Buddhists, and vice-versa.

Of course, the wars aren't just about theology. There is always territory and wealth attached, as so-called 'faith communities' turn their guiding myths into power and control. But what holds these groups together isn't just about land and money; it's about the absolute identification with one or another definition of truth. An "order of existence", as the definition tells us.

Belonging to a faith tradition, or religion, embraces the follower and enhances relationships with others who share their world view. At the same time, it makes non-believers into outsiders, makes them "heathen" or *"kafir"*, words in current use for "infidels". The sociologists refer to this as "in-group solidarity, out-group hostility". The next time you read about a war somewhere, in Sudan, in Syria or Iraq, be sure that what lies at its core is the clash of world views, out-groups reacting with hostility to each other.

In most of the world, religion is unquestioned. In many places, it's illegal to doubt the received theology. If you marry someone from the out-group, you might wind up in jail, or worse. If you're openly gay in Iran or Saudi Arabia, you're toast. Now the net is closing in places like Uganda and Nigeria, as we know all too well from the gay and lesbian refugee support groups recently formed in London. The evidence for punishing gay people springs from – where else? – The Bible. Also the Quran. Holy books, scriptures that are thought to be infallible, are the licences to behave inhumanely. And not just "over there". We well-fed Western democracies have had our share of persecution – too much to mention. And we're not alone. Here's another nugget from Wikipedia:

The last person in Britain to be sent to prison for blasphemy was John William Gott, on 9 December 1921. He had three previous convictions for blasphemy when he was prosecuted for publishing two pamphlets entitled Rib Ticklers, or Questions for Parsons and God and Gott. In these pamphlets Gott satirised the biblical story of Jesus entering Jerusalem, comparing Jesus to a circus clown. He was sentenced to nine months' hard labour despite suffering from an incurable illness, and died shortly after he was released. The case became the subject of public outrage.

Thank God for public outrage, huh? What that says is that a modern, secular society was getting started about a hundred years ago. In a secular society, you should be able to pooh-pooh the religious books that turn the world's religious people into wearers of intellectual strait jackets. But drawing cartoons of the Prophet can still get you killed, as the Charlie Hebdo magazine staff found out.

I'm always interested in talking to people who resettle in Britain from other countries that are not so liberal. I have talked to dozens – Iranians, Africans, Pakistanis and Afghanis, to name a few – who have left behind their home places. I find two things. One is a kind of nostalgia, or homesickness, for the remembered sense of certainty and welcome of the familiar. Sometimes they continue to dress in a way reminiscent of their origins. They know where to get the food that they are used to, because London really is a cosmopolitan city.

The other thing I find is that, despite the awful tales of youth radicalisation in the direction of Islamist terrorism, many of them have gradually adopted a more liberal way of looking at the world. Last week I had a Ugandan taxi driver, and I told him that I was working with a number of gay Ugandans who had had to leave their homes for fear of persecution. I was testing him a bit, I confess. He frowned, and I thought, *Here we go. I'm going to get a song and dance about gay sex being wrong.* But instead he said, 'Why can't people just be in love with whoever they want?' I nearly applauded. I went on: 'How do you feel about gay people?' He shrugged. 'They do their way, and I do mine. What's it to me?'

I wanted to write a poem or symphony when he said that. I wanted to say, do you realise how precious that insight is? How much it means for the future of humanity? That it's proof that little by little, through struggle and war, we might be learning the real Golden Rule: "Live and let live"?

So, I say religion is bad because it seeks to deny that insight. The Anglican Church is tearing itself apart over gay clergy and women bishops. The struggle is fascinating to watch. The insights of a liberal secular consciousness are at it, hammer and tongs, with the kind of belief that comes from a book, suspect in origin and clearly out of date. In religion, it seems, it's not enough to believe something yourself; you have to make sure everyone else does too.

I say religion is bad because it fosters narrow identification with a circle that, by definition, excludes others. The TV channels are full of discussions about why a well-educated boy, born and raised in Brick Lane, wants to go and fight as a jihadi in a place he has never seen. If you ask, that boy will say, 'Because they are invading our lands and killing our brothers.' You might then ask, 'Are they really invading East London? And why are your brothers some people you don't know, whose language you don't speak, and not some guy named Joe Bloggs who is a fellow West Ham supporter?' The answer is obvious; you are defined by your religion. You *are* your religion.

If that's a bit confusing, please note that I didn't say that spiritual search is bad. I didn't say that there is no truth worth turning over every single rock to find, and celebrate, and proclaim. What I am saying is that there is no possibility of committing the whole truth to a creedal statement. There are no beliefs that must be adhered to before you can be saved. And that truth can come from any direction, dragged out of any religion, or none.

So I don't think I belong to a religion. I think I'm happy to join a meeting point for people whose longing for truth has brought them into contact with others. The others may not share any beliefs in common that one has come up with over a lifetime of reflection. But we band together, we few – we very few – because we have a very strict requirement for truth. It's not enough to hear the words of others or to read passages from a magical handbook. Any truth we accept has to be born and reared in our own minds and hearts, following our own time.

There's one more thing. I have argued with religious people about this quite a lot. I say that we agnostic seekers are the ones who genuinely trust that there is a binding, creative force in the universe, which many are happy to call God. We think that, if we're sincere, that that force or spirit or God will make use of our confusion and our doubt. If we're truthful, we cannot be wrong. There will be no narrow gate we have to squeeze through, and no absurdities we have to live by.

Religion? No thanks.

Chilli is the Truth

Not long ago I made a chilli con carne, something I like to think I do pretty well, and I remembered a country boy who ate in my Mexican restaurant years ago. When I asked him if he had enjoyed his meal, he said, 'Mmmm, I'll tell you what, friend. That chilli is the *truth*.'

I think that's funny because it's ridiculous. Chilli con carne may be a lot of things, but it's hardly the truth. The truth is, well, something more ... sublime, maybe? How would you define it? A dictionary will give you synonyms like accuracy, precision, candour, faith and honesty. Certain philosophers, notably Aristotle, define it as the opposite of falsehood, which is fine, except then you have to know what falsehood is. The Internet will give you 103,768,109 websites about truth, but you don't have to open more than a dozen or so to realise that nobody knows what truth is, but most are keen to display their version of it. You can run your mouse all day and not get a lot closer.

Children seem fairly interested in the truth, at least at first. They get handed so many watered-down versions of reality, who can blame them? The first time you see Santa's bounty hidden in the garage two weeks before Christmas, or the tooth fairy trips over your discarded jumper and curses just like your father does before going back to watch the late movie, a germ of truth begins to penetrate the sweet flannel of childhood. When Great-Grandma has a funeral and grownups are seen weeping, even though "Great-Grandma is up in heaven with God, Dear," truth can be glimpsed peering around the edges of life.

Soon enough, though, truth begins to be a simple matter of learning and memorising the accepted responses to things. As you grow up, you begin to take pride in forming opinions just like, or directly opposite to, those of your parents. Then you encounter the fashionable, and you conspire with your peers to believe certain things and act in a certain way. The world becomes a series of exams, just like in school, and you just have to swot up a bit. By the time you're twenty or so, you've got it all sorted, and you wonder how your parents can have attained vast age without knowing much of anything, really.

Then it may happen –it nearly always does – that something makes you restless. You can think of it as hormonal, like getting wisdom teeth, or you can see it as the inevitable preoccupation of a conscious being, but learning the truth begins to re-emerge as an issue. The accepted formulae don't seem enough. You might start to have children, and they might start asking hard questions. Someone youngish, your own age, dies, and the impossible becomes possible, even likely. Once in a while the emptiness of your carefully collected opinions and stored up answers becomes painfully visible. Some of us start about then on a version of what truth seekers have always called a path of discovery.

The first place you're likely to look is in the tradition out of which you sprang. If you grew up a Presbyterian or a Jew, you might feel the urge to re-examine some of the ideas you had already heard and put aside.

About that time you might start looking for truth in some unorthodox places. Reading Erich von Daneken, say, and seeing human origins as seeds sown by intergalactic visitors with god-like wisdom and intelligence. Or finding that a macrobiotic diet is a precondition to self-realisation. You might find others like yourself – other scientologists or kundalini yoga disciples, with whom you can share the excitement of truth made easy. Or, Heaven forfend, you might get born again. When that happens, there is a fleeting sense of certainty about life. You just need to get rid of your "engrams" or attain the next level of yogic initiation, and the vanished sense of having everything sussed out that you lost when you left your first youth seems to be yours again.

Then you might start to look around at your colleagues, and see that they have become a little, well, fanatical. They go about with a supercharged glow that goes along with a direct line to truth. If you get into a conversation, you might find them a bit elusive, as if their truth was a well-kept secret. You might notice that they sometimes exchange knowing glances that make you feel slightly creepy. If you get involved in something like this, you have to keep reminding yourself all the time about it. If you can't find a parking space, there is a theological code you can consult that will explain it. You might find yourself getting anxious, because the effort of squeezing the whole great chaotic smorgasbord of life into a theory is a lot of work. You may be like many people whose gift for life makes them poorly equipped for fanaticism and then fall out of your truth into the complexities of life once again.

It may be that now the search for truth becomes more intellectual. Great writers and teachers have filled tomes with records of their own searches for millennia. Maybe you'll home in on philosophy and make the search one of thought process. You may find an affinity with the Epicureans of ancient Greece or do some existential breast-beating with Soren Kierkegaard. Truth becomes a much-loved preoccupation here, and the way to it is through logical argument. The mind is the instrument by which truth can be apprehended, whether it is glorious or hopeless. You began to search for truth in order to satisfy some soulful need; reducing it to a pattern of mere theory may be unfulfilling, like yesterday's chewing gum. As each succeeding bright idea floats into consciousness, it seems to bring with it new possibilities for emptiness. The deconstructionists of the post-modern movement have all but spoiled the game: there can be no truth worth searching for. At best a series of situational truths that depend more upon the questioner than the question, making proponents like Michel Foucault even deny that what he was doing was philosophy. Truth is either unavailable or non-existent, philosophically speaking. And so it may be that the search is derailed again, and what ensues is a kind of expectant vacuum.

Meanwhile, life hasn't stopped. The lawn grows inexorably, and the white hairs appear around your ears as if by magic. Sometimes you feel good about things, and sometimes you don't. Sometimes you have the feeling that there is something quite magical happening just outside your line of vision, and sometimes a shaft of evening sunlight on a stand of poplar trees seems to hold an encoded version of the truth. Sometimes, for no reason at all, you feel that, whether you can explain it or not, everything is somehow all right.

Maybe that guy who liked my chilli wasn't all that far wrong after all. Maybe the truth isn't something you learn or think, but something you experience. The Rabbi Jesus had some interesting things to say about that. In contrast to his predecessor, Aristotle, Jesus didn't have a relativistic definition of truth. It was not just the opposite of falsehood, in fact not a concept at all: it was an experience. He said, "I am the truth."

This puts a slightly different slant on things. All this time we had been looking, to paraphrase the country and western song, in all the wrong places. We had been thinking that truth was something to be understood, not something to simply be. That's because we didn't listen carefully enough to the great heroes of consciousness. Wanting to arrive at the threshold of eternity dragging that limited but much-loved thing called the mind is like trying to leapfrog over your own back.

Jesus wasn't alone in this. The great sages, from Krishna to Hafiz to Hildegard of Bingen, all had the same thing to say. Truth is something that has to do with realisation in the sense of *making real,* not in the sense of an intellectual *Eureka!* Finding the truth, we have been told repeatedly, though ignoring it all the while, is finding one's real self. Those who have found themselves in this way often become gurus or saints, not through any craftiness on their parts, but because they are so different from everybody else that you can't help noticing it. Becoming established in the truth has a certain quality to it, a quality of being that is unmistakable. If you've never met anyone like that, make an effort. I have, and I'll just have to ask you to take my word for it.

Not everyone attains to the spiritual greatness of the prophets – at least, not all at once. It is a gradual process of uncovering from the dust and rubble of one's own experience the truth where it touches us. I have known some great people who would shudder at the thought of being called a saint, but who, nonetheless, have emanated that certain quality of being. I'm sorry I can't be more precise than that. And I have known some quite ordinary people who from time to time have shown flashes of this quality associated with living in the truth. These too are people who, in one way or another, are "telling the truth", even if their words are clumsy and their study of philosophy inadequate. We are engaged in nothing here if we are not engaged in that – the "telling" of the truth that defies the cleverness of the mind and even the determination of the will.

Those people who are most gifted with the spontaneous experience of the truth have certain characteristics, and so I would recommend that anyone who wants to be like them imitate these. This is not an exhaustive list, but it's what I have come to believe, and it's the way I'd like to live myself, if I wasn't so lazy.

These people have little of what we call "attitude." That is, their opinions are either constantly subject to re-evaluation, or else they don't bother with them at all. This makes them easy to be around, and you find yourself wanting to talk to them. They laugh easily, but not only at cleverness. It's a shame that in their zeal to nail Jesus down theologically that the apostles didn't let his fun-loving nature shine through a bit more. Still, if you look for it, you'll find it.

These people have a quality of what Ram Dass calls "being here now." They are with you physically, and they are fully rooted in the world where water is wet and salt is salty, not "otherworldly" and over-spiritual. You can see them enjoying food and drink, but just as easily able to forego it, without any sense of compulsion.

These people never need to be psychologically accommodated. There are no taboo subjects, no tip-toeing around areas where there might be issues buried like land mines. When you are with them, you can be yourself, which, of course, means that they are evoking a sense of self-revelation in you.

The final thing – the main thing, really – is that you love them. They are not necessarily pretty or ugly, powerful or weak. They are just they, and in being who they are, make you more like your own real self. This is the feeling of love and connectedness, and it can only be invoked by those whose nature is in itself loving.

To the extent that we are like this, we are close to that thing we have been looking for in cults and books and chilli con carne; the truth. We can't explain it, because it is beyond all explanation. We can't set out on a diet or exercise programme and attain it, because it lies not just at the end of striving, but also at the point before striving begins. We can just wait for it, knowing that it is our birth-right and the true art of each one of us, however lost we may sometimes feel.

And that's the truth.

Why Snowmen Have to Melt

Jesus of Nazareth was probably a difficult guy to be around. I've already given some of the reasons why I say this. But he wasn't the only one.

Read the biography of the Hindu saint Ramakrishna some time. Read between the lines in Buddhist scripture and find the same wacky behaviour. If you want to go looking in Islam, there is plenty of material in the Koran, but the Sufis will give you a proper diet of the oddness of saints. The thing that links them all is just one fact: they were all acting according to the rules of an invisible world, and to the rest of us it looks like plain old lunacy.

It seems that there is something we aren't able to see, but which has its own alternative logic. Things like, "Love your enemies," (don't spend the world's wealth on more and more nuclear weapons). "Forgive sinners," (don't strap them to a medical table and lethally inject them). "Take no heed of the morrow," (insurance policies and retirement schemes aren't the answer). This invisible world, wherever and whatever it is, is topsy-turvy. Or maybe, turvy-topsy.

Realising this, we have got two choices. One, dismiss what these voices have been telling us through the centuries, cobble together some pale logic like, "Well, that was then; things are more complicated these days." Or, two, let the riddle do its work on us. Let it be cause for second thoughts as we pass our days getting and spending, make us more ready to stop and listen the next time we pass somebody talking to themselves in public.

One way I am able to get a small insight into the odd logic of the saints is through something Meher Baba once said. Responding to a question about the importance of worldly institutions, he said that all projects, even the grandest and most benevolent, were nothing more than a temporary scaffolding erected during the building of an invisible reality. I take this to mean that however strong your ambitions, for good or selfish purposes, and however well-established your success may be in the eyes of the world, everything is temporary. Not only temporary, but somehow short of the mark. That means governments, great works of art, noble buildings, and – yes – religions, too. What we call religion, after all, is only a time-based view of things, ready to vanish as has every symbol yet invented.

An image that helps me with this idea of the invisible reality is that of a couple of children making a snowman. They are getting bits of coal for the eyes and a carrot for the nose and begging old scarves and hats off the neighbours. They are totally engrossed in the project. Their mother watches them indulgently. She has heard the weather report on TV and knows that the cold snap is ending, that during the night old Frosty will become a sodden lump, the carrot snatched by some opportunistic passing bird. So why doesn't she tell them just to save themselves time and disappointment and come in and watch TV instead?

She doesn't because she knows that their experience of the snowman is important. She sees their dedication and their enjoyment, and it gives her pleasure, or even hope. If she is especially wise, she will know that what is happening is more than mere fantasy. The kids are learning about human anatomy. They are trying themselves out as creative beings, learning about art. They are learning co-operation with someone else. They are merging with their environment in a way which she, perhaps, cannot. All this is going on while the mercury rises in the thermometer, and it doesn't matter. The archetype of *snowmanness* is alive and well in this generation.

Great masters have often used a similar metaphor to explain their own working with disciples. Just as we know that the snowman is melting, they know that *everything* is melting: careers, wealth, societies, families, religions. Some of them tell us this in no uncertain terms. One version of the Buddha's last words goes like this: "All things are in a state of decomposition; therefore pursue your own salvation with diligence." Jesus, questioned at his trial, said it perhaps more pithily, "My kingdom is not of this world." Plato's Socrates remained unruffled because of his imperishable *ideal.* All of them seem to agree that, although our snowmen are impermanent, they are not without value; they point to something invisible and permanent.

Where is this imperishable reality, then? Let's go back to the children. Their experience is not far removed from our own. Their fingers are getting stiff and their noses ruddy. They share our world, where salt is salty and water is wet, but they do not share our reality. We have grown beyond the time-bound focus of the snowman moment. Our experience, our more developed intellects tell us that what is being built will soon disappear, but that there is still something wonderful about watching Frosty's rebirth in the front garden. If we had to explain it to them, we would probably say that they would understand when they were older, as we have done.

One of the saints listed above might say the same thing. In fact, many have. Seeing our projects come and go, they see through the moment to another reality – you might say "another kingdom." They inhabit our world, are subject to poison and nails through the wrists, but their reality is somewhere far removed from our limited concerns. They know that, just as the kids will mature into indulgent parents, so will we all one day see something of the invisible reality that gives us life. And that getting there means building snowmen and watching them melt.

If everything is just scaffolding for something much more real being built, it has some lessons for us. It invites detachment from success and failure, for one thing. Part of the lesson is the snowman melting, after all. Knowing it will melt, that all our earthly hopes, our striving for second-hand immortality through achievement, fame and wealth will all melt too is a good touchstone for us as we learn and grow. Maybe also, the image of the scaffold will make us more tender towards others in their ambitions and grasp of power. Even better, we might be able to forgive ourselves.

Most of all, though, remembering this may tune our senses to the real behind the ordinary. The hard slog of days has a different flavour when viewed as a preliminary to understanding. If we know we can look forward to finding in the ashes of our hopes a glimpse of the miraculous, we may gradually start watching and listening for the truth in ways we can't just now. But we have reason to believe – good reason to believe – that it is on its way.

Canon John's Window

It seems I'm being controversial again. Despite my good intentions to just tend my little garden of liberal flowers and coast into a quiet retirement, my big mouth has got in my way again.

One day I got a telephone call from a reporter on the local newspaper. He was following up on a same-sex marriage debate we hosted in May. He said he was doing a survey of churches in town about the upcoming legislation concerning the rights of gay and lesbian couples to marry. He quoted a Roman Catholic priest, a guy who teaches religious education in six local schools and has a big church in a suburb. He had recently said that the whole issue of gay marriage was "unwelcome" and contradicted the teachings of the Bible.

As you can imagine, I scoffed at that. We Unitarians have been scoffing at bullying nonsense for a few centuries now. It is important to be as polite as possible, probably, whilst being sure not to lose the energy of the scoff.

Last weekend's paper quoted me as saying that the priest's position was "ignorant". I actually said the position was one of ignorance, and that in fifty years' time we would be incredulous to hear that we had ever entertained any idea of trying to stifle any expression of love and commitment freely given. I said that such remarks as he made did more harm than good and that the church leaders who made statements like that needed to have their knuckles rapped from time to time.

We Unitarian ministers in the UK have got a little chat room. Really just a closed email group, where we ask and give advice, spread pernicious gossip, lament the passing of the good old days, and keep ourselves amused. I don't use it much, but I did send in a link to the newspaper article to my colleagues, to hear what they had to say.

Most of the responses were favourable, but some of them said that they thought that I should be more "temperate" in my choice of words. Presumably, this is because in lots of places our ministers are trying to get some sort of limited acceptance from the local councils of Christian churches. This means they are extremely loth to cause any form of consternation or offence, no matter how mild and no matter how deserving.

I can understand their points of view. Because of what I view as an overly obsessive concern for numbers of pew sitters, one of our favoured recruitment techniques seems to be to make oneself as mild and agreeable as everyone else, as if to say, "Really, we're just like all those other churches; we just have modernised hymns and one less creed to memorise."

This ploy is doomed on two counts. One, the other churches are emptying out as rapidly as ours are – maybe even faster. And two: unless there is something striking and unusual about a church, something that makes the people who would rather loll about with the papers on a Sunday morning get up and go to a service, we are out of options anyway.

We Unitarians were once very unpopular with the church establishment. Yes, even more than we are now. We were called Unitarians as a form of mockery, just as Quakers were called by that name instead of the Society of Friends. We were famously called "a feather bed for the fallen" by a well-known Anglican priest. Even more, we were forced to build our churches five miles from a town's market cross, or to stash them in yards invisible from the street. And sometimes we got jailed or even burnt at the stake. Strangely enough, our pews were filled. They were filled with thinking people, people for whom the prevailing logic of society wasn't convincing. I suppose "temperate language" was less of an issue back in those days.

This isn't really an issue about gay rights, you know. As Elton John said in a recent *Guardian* article, this is about human rights. It doesn't matter whether you like or dislike gay people, or whether you approve or disapprove of what gay people do. It doesn't even matter if you think gay marriage should NOT be legalised; that's a matter of your own conscience and due to your own tastes and upbringing in the first place.

I'll try a little experiment. I'm going to quote Ben Summerskill, who is the director of the gay rights organisation Stonewall. This quote appeared in all the papers at the time that a Scottish Cardinal was making such a huge fuss about the proposed marriage legalisation, decrying it as "un-

Christian". Summerskill said, "If the Cardinal has a problem with same-sex marriage, he should probably avoid marrying someone of the same sex." If you think that's amusing, and even telling about certain attitudes, I'm delighted. I doubt very much that the priest in the nearby suburb would chuckle, or even get the point.

But I don't hate or even dislike those guys in the funny hats, who believe they hold the keys to the Kingdom of Heaven. As a sort of religious guy myself, I do understand that if my conception of the Holy were mocked, I would get upset. The problem is that for the devout believer, boundaries are set very far from their own concerns. They feel that it is their job to make everyone see the truth of their position. When that is frustrated, they get angry. They can make bigoted remarks, conspire in oppressive legislation, even start the odd Inquisition, as we know from history.

When the fervour to preserve a certain version of religious truth gets out of hand, it can make others suffer. When the Catholic Church in Ireland is able for many years to prohibit the sales of contraceptives, they cause needless suffering, and even death from the resort of ordinary people to dangerous abortions. When the Pope forbids birth control in funds sent to Africa, an epidemic of AIDS results. That's the time to forget about mild ecumenical wishes and shove a spanner into the machinery. And that's where tolerance finds its natural limit.

I had a chance to think this all over one morning when I was in a taxi. Where else? The driver had actually seen the newspaper article and was keen to talk to me about it. He's a kind of natural philosopher. He's full of ideas that come from a range of sources, including philosophical tomes and Chinese fortune cookies. He's also a proud atheist, as he spends much time reminding me. I don't mind; I'm tolerant.

He began ranting about the foolish churchmen that wave the Bible at everyone, even though hardly anybody is paying attention. He was so harsh in his judgements that I found myself inching toward the position of the cardinals and their protestant counterparts. I told him that each of these guys who now find themselves on a shrinking ice floe of old-fashioned dogma got there the hard way, through having a powerful vision of the truth. When some old boy in a brocaded robe jabs his finger at the sinful world, he is trying to protect the very thing that gives his life meaning. He may be wrong, he may even be stupid, but he is inwardly heroic.

Later I thought about what I should have said to the taxi driver. I missed my chance, so I'll tell you instead.

Once upon a time, say, you looked out of a window and saw something so beautiful and so utterly life-changing that it made you devote your entire life to it. Jesus passing by, maybe. This vision just had to be shared, so you found yourself in the company of those who happened to have been looking out of the same window at the same time.

You went back and kept peeking out of the window, but then you started to get it wrong. You decorated the window with as much lovely material as you were capable of. You gilded the frame and surrounded it with murals. Then you placed panes of stained glass in the opening, with marvellous figures, depicting the scene as you saw it. The window became the centre of a movement, then a group, finally an organisation. All your attention was directed toward this window and its wonderful, elaborate message.

That's why you weren't able to see through the glass the next time something wonderful and life-changing passed by.

As much as I think I'd like to dismiss that priest as a mere bigot and fool, I'm afraid I can't. You see, he's being heroic. He's defending the one and only truth as it occurred to him. Guys like him wound up being burnt at the stake, too. I sometimes wonder what would happen if I got trapped in a lift with someone like Canon John. When they came to rescue us, hours later, would we be at each other's throats or in each other's arms? Could I sway him with my clever words and my nice personality, or would we be captaining some opposing South London armies?

I know that Canon John is gazing lovingly at that stained-glass window that keeps any recent revelations of truth from getting through. My question is: what is the best way to get that window opened again? Talk him into dismantling it with temperate words, or, as some people think I did, chuck a brickbat right through it?

And besides, hasn't Canon John given me a good life lesson?

We religious liberals need to remember this: let's be sure we don't get into making our own opaque window glass, lest we miss something wonderful and life-changing as it passes by.

Who Wants to Know?

Do you ever watch daytime quiz programmes? Go on – you can confess if you do. I often watch the version of *Deal or No Deal* that comes on at 5 pm, unless, of course, I'm somewhere else toiling away in the fields of the Lord.

If you do watch them, you'll realise that the producers think it's terribly important, for some reason, for each contestant to give a potted biography of themselves before they go after the prizes. I suppose this adds a bit of human interest to the game and keeps people watching so that the ads for insurance comparison sites and vacuum cleaners have lots of viewers.

I've observed that the men who play these games most often start by saying what they do for a living. The unknown person then becomes known to us as a bricklayer or a sales manager. The women, though, tend to describe themselves in terms of their families, so that in a short while we know how many children they have and how long they've been married. Not always, but often.

This difference reflects the findings of a sociological study made in the 1960s. The subjects were children in a primary school playground. They were observed while playing some game or other and recorded on camera. The results were interesting: the boys, as it turned out, were mostly concerned with the game, the score, the winners and losers. The girls, on the other hand, were mostly concerned with the relationships between the players. This gave rise to the conclusion that males are more interested in task and achievement, and that females consider human interaction and relationship – you might say the human stories – more crucial.

Whether this is a genetic trait or an acquired one is not known. Since then, with many more women rightfully demanding access to careers and many more men interested in developing their "female sides", things may have changed. That particular box has always seemed too tight-fitting for my liking. But what is interesting to me is the process of self-identification. When asked the question, "Who are you?" the first reaction will be to tell a short tale about oneself: "I'm an architect", "I'm a mother of three", etc.

If you have excelled at something, the answers become even more specific: "She's a Booker Prize-winning author"; "He's an MP". The story becomes more dramatic, and more specific. If you're famous, the story is already known to many people. Brad Pitt is divorced from Angelina Jolie, having divorced Jennifer Aniston earlier. Lord Archer is a pulp novelist and an ex-con.

But however well-known one's story is, the result is the same: we are our stories. At least, that's what we think. But there are deeper and more challenging ways to answer the question, "Who am I?"

Western philosophy has always tended toward the idea that there is a basic self, usually seen as the mind. Rene Descartes produced his famous rabbit out of a hat by saying those lines, "I think, therefore I am." This idea implies that, at our most basic, we are the mind, and that the body is somehow separate from this. This is dualism, the fundamental split in the human being that has spawned all sorts of fancies in medicine, law and politics. It is sometimes referred to the "the ghost in the machine" – the mind riding around in a body it is not very firmly anchored to.

This idea of a core somebody that exists in all of us was investigated by the Buddha. After many years of meditation, it is said, he reached a state of "no mind", in which he was able to see that there is no unique, individual self at all, but series of reactions to stimuli, much as a nerve reacts to being pressed. His solution was to attain a state of non-existence, which represented freedom from this cause-and-effect process and attaining Nirvana. Or, as some believe, basically ceasing to exist.

As much as I feel drawn to the peacefulness and gentleness of Buddhism, that idea has always bothered me. Maybe it's the screaming of my tiny ego, that little man who wants to say, "But I DO exist!" Maybe that's why I have always felt much more strongly drawn to other eastern voices, those who speak of the soul.

The problem with the idea of the soul is that you can't find it anywhere connected to an organ in the human body. The mind, say scientists, is a series of neural connections in the brain. You can watch it work if you're willing to attach electrodes or saw through the skull. The soul, though, is more elusive, if it exists. Some scientists, happily at play in a God-free and totally material universe, think that one day they'll find a little gland, called the "God spot" and explain all this nonsense about the soul away, once and for all.

I once attended a meeting of followers of an Indian spiritual master. The speaker was a psychologist who had worked closely with Timothy Leary, the guru of LSD fame, and Richard Alpert, now known as the teacher Baba Ram Dass. During the talk, the speaker asked us to do a little exercise. We were sitting quietly, and he asked us to become as aware of our bodies as we could. It was quite thorough; he even took us through the digestive tract. Then he said suddenly, 'Who's watching?' Meaning that since we were able to monitor our bodily sensations, we should know who was doing that.

'The mind,' was the answer from us in the audience. The speaker smiled. 'Good,' he said. Then he took us down a different path of meditation, or reflection or whatever. We were asked to observe our thoughts as they came and went, something that is routine in a certain kind of meditation. We sat quietly and watched ourselves thinking this and that, becoming aware of the process in the same way we had been with the observation of the body. Then he said, suddenly, 'Who's watching?'

It was a bit startling to me. I got his point at once. If I am my mind, how can I observe with it at the same time? It seemed to me that there must be another "me" that was not exactly what I think of as my conscious mind at all, but something much more basic. This was somehow a core "observer me", something that underlies the ebb and flow of thoughts and sensations.

Sceptics might say that this was nothing more than a separate region of the brain. But it didn't feel like that at all. It felt somehow very familiar and comfortable, as if – whoever it was that was doing the observation – I knew how to be that as well. In fact, it seemed to remind me of moments throughout my life, usually accidental moments, in which the "observer me" was close at hand. Especially in childhood, in those moments of lying in the grass with nothing in particular to do and nowhere in particular to go, when I rested in this "observer me" as if I had always been there.

One morning I awoke in my bed and had a momentary lack of memory of where I was. Not just where I was, but *who* I was. You'd think that this would be terrifying, as stories about amnesia often are. But it wasn't. I felt absolutely at home and peaceful, and the only thing I could come up with in answer to the question "Who am I?" was "I am consciousness."

In that moment, the story by which I usually define myself had been lost or abandoned. If Noel Edmunds had asked me who I was, I couldn't have told him. And I knew: I only pretend to be the character in my personal story. I am really someone much bigger, much older and – yes – much more at home than that.

So the question "Who are you?" has got a twist in the tale. You can call it the "observer self" or "consciousness" or even, to save breath, the soul. What that means, or could mean, if we had the will and the courage, is that we could learn to live in that condition. If we did, we wouldn't be afraid of anything, not even death. We would act a lot more caring and gentle towards others, because we would not just believe that they were somehow the same as us, but *experience* it as well. The stories we tell ourselves about our lives, about how we are victims or heroes or this or that, would seem pretty meaningless. We would be a lot like Jesus and the other great spiritual heroes, in fact.

That would be great, wouldn't it? But there's just one little problem: how do we get from where we are, the chess pieces in our little stories, to that state of awareness?

I have a good friend who has spent his life wrestling with that question. He has written a book, in Spanish, because he's a Venezuelan, about his struggles to get back to a state of awareness he once reached during a mystical experience. He has been through gurus like most of us go through socks. He has lived in ashrams, spent long periods in India, read all of the spiritual literature available in paperback, fasted, lived on pennies. He seems to have reached a condition of calm now. Maybe it's age. But I get the impression that he has moved into still waters from the turbulence of his search.

And without double-guessing his unique state of mind, I think he's done something that I think we all must do. I think he's realised that it doesn't really matter if he can't access that state of soul awareness whenever he wants to. That there's no magic lantern that can be rubbed to produce it. I think he's realised, as I think we all might do, that if that is the "real" or the "realer" you, then it exists whether you experience it or not. Yes, it would be lovely never to have fear or anxiety or the disappointment of frustrated desires. But if you know – really know – that the insights of that higher version of yourself are true, then you need only content yourself with the knowledge. And know that, as I am accused of saying all the time, everything is all right. My theology, maybe in a nutshell: everything is somehow, counter-intuitively, incredibly, *all right.*

Because we don't seem to be able to remember that all the time, we can just try to relax with the knowledge that we sometimes *do* know it. And maybe sometimes, in a moment of meditation or wafted on the notes of a song, we might just sense the true answer to that question written in every heart.

Who am I? Who is asking the question? There's your answer.

Bark if You Believe

There are all sorts of theology out there these days. You have a whole Chinese menu to choose from, with the same problems those huge menus cause: when there's too much choice, you simply lose your appetite. Go down the list with me: narrative theology, process theology, liberation theology, feminist theology, natural theology, systematic theology, historical theology, practical theology, Biblical theology … the head swims.

The other day I came upon one that I really like. It's called "redneck theology". Here's an outline:

God loves you, so He makes it likely that you'll burn in Hell.
Sex is dirty and vile, so save it for the one you really love.

Yippee! Give me that old-time religion. We laugh now, but it was just such paradoxes that made me and my friends into junior atheists when we reached our teen years. It was bold, modern and a bit transgressive. We refused to say the Lord's Prayer in school assemblies. We would drive out to Moon Lake at night and drink cans of strong beer and talk about sex, art, sex, politics, sex and religion. And sex.

My mother didn't know it, but I had put away all that stuff and nonsense I got from Riverside Presbyterian Church about Jesus and Heaven and – above all – sin. The future stretched away as a seemingly infinite amount of time, and even once when a guy my age water-skied into a dock and was killed, we all secretly knew that we were, if not immortal, then at least safe from ordinary death. The medics would come up with something to prevent all that. Life was going to be great, and even greater because we were leaving behind superstition. There was no cosmic rule book, and no God sitting in judgment on us.

I can remember the glow of freedom that I felt then. But, like the chewing gum on the bedpost, it lost its flavour overnight. About the time

I got to those years when you stop knowing everything there is to know, new questions began to disturb me.

After treading the familiar route through reading D T Suzuki, various gurus, sitting in Zen meditation and a long detour through a course of psychedelic drugs, I finally found myself back at the beginning. I was stuck with a single word, one which I hate to use, even now. You know the one I mean: *faith.*

Mostly, when people use that word, they mean something like swallowing your reason, putting your mind to sleep and hypnotising yourself into a kind of feeble belief structure that relies on denial to exist. Come on – we don't want brainwashing; we want proof. We inhabit a scientific age. We've grown up from the Dark Ages. Faith, schmaith.

I would have felt the same way about it if I hadn't been forced into a Bible studies course in ministry training, when I finally found something that made sense to me. It was in the Book of Hebrews, which used to be ascribed to Paul, but was actually written three hundred years after his death. It is sometimes called the Unitarian book because it does away with a lot of the folderol from the earlier epistles. In chapter 11, it says:

"Now faith is the substance of things hoped for, the evidence of things unseen."

That put a different face on things, at least for me. The writer of that book was saying that faith had nothing to do with shaky belief structures. It was "substance". My online dictionary defines that word as:

"the real physical matter of which a person or thing consists and which has a tangible, solid presence."

And it is evidence:

"the available body of facts or information indicating whether a belief or proposition is true or valid."

Well and good. But where is this substance and this evidence? We can inquire back at the beginning of Western thought. Socrates used to talk about how most people were capable of hearing the muses speak to them. Not aloud, of course, but in an inner way. For muses read "the spirit". What the muses told them was what made a life into more than a passing series of events. Their singing granted the most important gift; *meaning.* But not everyone could hear or even wanted to listen for the muses. These people he called the *eu-a-moussoi,* or people content to live without a finely tuned inner connection with a reality that lies beyond the tedious succession of happenings that added up to nothing.

That means that all of us might have the ability to listen for the muses. Call it that if you like, or go Biblical and say the "still small voice". Or maybe the word I use in place of the scary word "faith", a *hunch.*

If the muses, or the Holy Spirit, are speaking to us, why can't we hear it all the time? As with most complex problems, there is no answer in kind. That is, there is no way to address a problem that has become so convoluted simply by subjecting it to the echo chamber of the mind.

For me, it would require something more than theory, and certainly more than the sort of fairy tale religion we got fed as kids. For me, it would have to be a perception, something that actually does speak to us through the cacophony of ideas that flutter around us like startled birds. Something, you might say, like the referee's whistle when a foul is committed on the football field.

Something, maybe, like a dog whistle. Can you hear it? The whistle doesn't make a sound, does it? We are fully aware, thinking people. We know when something exists for real and when it doesn't. Just like our friends, the ones I am always seeming to mock, but not really, the scientists. They will tell you that if something cannot be observed, cannot be weighed and measured, then it cannot exist. That's what happened to poor old God. They went looking for Him up in space and He wasn't there. They've been digging around in chunks of meat in the human brain and didn't find Him there, either.

And you know what? They're right, while being wrong. What they haven't taken into account, it seems to me, is the little matter of consciousness. We can only see what we have the equipment to see. We can only hear what we have the equipment to hear. We can only know what our limited brains can handle, too.

A dog whistle emits sounds that exceed our human range of 20 to 20,000 hertz, or vibrations per second. The whistle is very loud, audible to a dog or cat at a distance of one mile, in fact. The fact that we hear nothing does not imply that the sound does not exist; I've been using mine to torment local dogs in my neighbourhood all week.

Now I've just made a claim. You have a choice: you can believe it or not. Some of you know me, and most of you don't. Maybe you think, *well, the guy IS a minister, after all, so he's probably not lying*. But you don't know if I am deluded, maybe. Or doing a well-intentioned trick out of some misguided notion that I am doing you good.

We are faced with the same choices when we read the words of those great souls, people like Socrates and Rumi and Jesus and Ramakrishna. You can't prove what they say is true or false. You can take it or leave it. But if you take it, then everything begins to change. You are faced with the possibility that there is a whole new world that you need to attend to.

Then you can look for evidence. You can ask other people if they can hear the whistle. You can look around and see if your collie cocks his ears at the sound and make inferences. Maybe you can pop it into a lab and try to measure the vibrations another way. What you cannot reasonably do is dismiss it as a childish myth.

But there is another way. You can learn to listen. When the frequency of the whistle gets tantalisingly close to our range, we can just about sense that a sound is being made. The closer we get to our range of hearing, the more likely it is that we can detect the sound. On the cusp of 20,000 Hz, we can begin to pick it up. Some of us will undoubtedly have a slightly more extended range than others and so can hear it before we can. It may be that some of us are more likely than others to pick up the sound of the muses singing, too. When Rumi tells us of something he sees and hears, it's probably a good idea to believe him. Maybe the same thing goes for shabby people talking aloud on the street. Listening is listening, after all.

But there are well-known ways of tuning in to the faint sounds of truth. When we have moments of intuition in meditation, or prayer, in a hymn, or even in a glimpse of sunlight out of our window, we can sense, without really seeing, that something is near. Something that we have never had to live without, that we could not live without. Something that has many names and none at all. Something that we can perceive, not merely theorise about. Something that makes faith an actuality, not a vain wish or, as some would try to tell us, a delusion.

It seems to me that it does boil down to a matter of consciousness. What are we aware of, and what goes unnoticed by us like passing scenery from a train window? If we could find a way to notice, really notice things, if we could find a way to listen when there is no audible sound, that would be the way to raise our consciousness. That's how we might learn to hear the muses sing.

So bark if you believe.

Six Degrees of Separation

One day, a few years ago, I was on my way to get new photos taken for my US passport. It was a calm, sunny day in South London. I was in the middle of the sidewalk looking for Snappy Snaps, when a young man on a bicycle swerved close to me, nearly hitting me. I jumped back and looked at him, expecting, I don't know, "Excuse me" or something like that. But he turned his head in my direction and spat, obviously on purpose, near my feet.

He was young, a black late-teenager, wearing a stylish baseball cap and a few shiny bits of bling. He rode off around a corner. I was feeling a number of emotions: anger, outrage, a dash of fear. But the overwhelming sense was one that I don't think has a name all to its own. My feelings were hurt. I went into Snappy Snaps and had my picture taken. I don't know if I was glowering; you can't really tell from the photo.

I went across the street to Piccolino's, my favourite little café. A cappuccino was what I needed. But I continued to re-play the scene over and over in my head.

Me and the kid. Yes, we're different. But why should that matter so much? Where does the anger come from? We both live in Croydon. We might even support the same football team. We might even want the same person in No 10 Downing Street.

Of course, I am white and he is black. The inherent privilege in my status may be invisible to me, but, we are assured, is NOT, to him. I am old, carrying a world view formed, more or less, in the past century. I was raised in America, in the most unapologetically racist part of it. We are only just beginning to understand how what is called "entitlement" manifests itself, even in brief encounters on the street.

Then there is the spectre of projection. His flat-brimmed baseball cap and jeans just barely clinging stylishly to his hips trigger a whole story. Here are some of the elements of that: Gangsta Rap, teenage stabbings, dangerous gangs outside fried chicken shops, likely macho abuse of girls, etc. The story unrolls almost like a scene in a movie. When that happens, you cannot see what is before your eyes. You cannot see the person at all.

But I'm not the only guilty party. Seeing me on the street, his own projection begins to stream. Old white guy, who probably uses the N-word with his mates down the pub. Friend of the police, Tory, or Republican, voter, blocking the pavement, oozing entitlement from his unstylish shirt to his horrible shoes.

What we were both doing is what is called "profiling", that thing that, in its worst form, leads to white policemen shooting African Americans, as we see in horrific YouTube clips. I couldn't see him, and he couldn't see me. The film took us both over.

Profiling is probably inevitable. Maybe it's wired into our genes. In an evolutionary context, being able quickly to determine exactly who is, and who isn't, a member of your tribe, would be an important survival mechanism. But when it comes to a modern, urban democracy, that survival mechanism ceases to be an advantage and becomes a fatal stumbling block.

I am not, by any reasonable definition, a racist. It wasn't that the guy was black per se; my dear ones in many countries have dark skin, including my friends sitting every Sunday in my church. It was a kind of cocktail of images that have sprung up in the cultural swamp of modern Britain. I have had similar encounters with pale-skinned and freckled kids, too. It was something just as insidious as racism, though we haven't come up with a name for it yet. It's something that now threatens us all, on both sides of the Atlantic. Something that divides us, and that has the potential to destroy all that we value.

At the moment, I can't speak to my own sister. She lives in Louisiana. She is a Republican, and I am not. At any earlier time of history, that wouldn't have made much difference. We might score points off each other in jokes or have a tense moment at Thanksgiving dinner. But things have changed: we have been forced, even though we went willingly, into two different tribes.

The things which separate us have become the building blocks of our personalities. They have started to determine who our friends are, what we read, how we spend our time. The extreme ends of our two-tribe world introduce more and more bizarre elements into our belief structures. I can't believe that she and her husband own several firearms. She can't believe that I am delighted to officiate at same-sex weddings. She thinks Obama was an agent of the so-called Deep State. I say that Trump is a moral idiot. Try having Thanksgiving dinner now.

Nobody is more politically opinionated than I – that's a confession. In my marrow, I believe that the policies I support and the underlying philosophy of fairness and respect for truth that animate them, are the only way forward for the human race. I cannot easily understand how anyone with even the barest grasp of logic can disagree with me.

But that's exactly what I have to do.

If I don't, then I am adding to the mad dance which, more than anything – global warming, North Korea, Putin or Covid-19 – threatens the future of the race. I am losing sight of my sister. She is vanishing over a horizon that did not exist when we were kids. My field of friendship is getting narrower as well. People who are like me are easy; everyone else is a problem.

As the tribes form and the battle lines are drawn outside, it is important to remember that there is no way to win. Our side can come out on top in an election or a referendum only to create, not the happy result we longed for, but the formation of permanent bitterness. In that sense, it does not matter whether we are in the 52 per cent or the 48. The limited victory will remain under threat. Rancour, nursed in defeat, is dangerous. After Obama's term finished, there was a remarkable, and horrifying, rise in racial crime. Many people believe that those who harbour racial hatred were steaming in silence during the term in office of a black president, and that his leaving popped open the pressure valve. The short-term gains in even the most important arenas – health care, immigration justice, fair wages – become vulnerable once the key players are off the board.

This where I'm supposed to tell you what we can do. It's considered bad ministry to lay a heavily prophetic sermon on a captive audience and just leave them hanging. Plus, it's rude. I've tried reading the websites of those who don't agree with me; even the Alt Right lunatic fringe. I don't think that's the way. You just find yourself screaming silently. And it goes without saying that the kind of Neo-Nazi groups that besieged Charlottesville are fully beyond the pale.

But I haven't told you the rest of the story.

After my brush with the young guy on the bike, I went into Piccolino's and ordered a cappuccino. I had fifteen minutes to wait for my photos. I ordered at the counter and then took a seat near the door. I looked briefly at my phone, as you do, then looked up to see the same young guy sitting not six feet away, eating a plate of scrambled eggs. I think our eyes locked at the same instant.

Without thinking, I said, 'Hey, man. How's your life?'

There was a second or two of hesitation, then he responded, 'Pretty good. How are you?'

Within a few minutes we were talking animatedly. He was impressed that I'm American and talked about wanting to go to Las Vegas. He had a job in a print shop, which he got after finishing school. The conversation was easy, and enjoyable. It went on through the eggs and the cappuccino, and when my fifteen minutes were up, I rose to leave. But we weren't finished, and the conversation went on when he mounted his bike outside. I felt genuinely reluctant to end the conversation. I know he did too. Finally he said, 'I better get to work,' and rode away.

I know – it's just anecdotal. But since that encounter, I've wondered about that young guy. I like him. I think that in some very small way, I understand him. I'd like to know if he's wondered about me, but it doesn't really matter if he hasn't. I feel that he may think, the next time he decides to offend an old white guy, that maybe he shouldn't. I know that the next time I'm inclined to dismiss someone because they're covered in bling, that I'll stop for a moment. And though I hesitate to introduce a Christian concept here, I have to say that the mood that descended onto both of us felt like grace. Undeserved, unpredictable grace.

Now I think the way forward lies in the microcosm. In fact, I believe that it is solely in the small contacts between human beings that change becomes possible. I won't be surprised if you think of this as just some wishful thinking. How can a single person, through limited interactions, make even a shred of difference against the background noise of war drums? And are you thinking I suggest that you give up your political dreams? Well, I'm not. I'm talking about making that which underlies and determines your political goals much closer than it seems right now.

Do you remember that game of a few years ago called "Six Degrees of Separation"? It started as a kind of joke, to prove that everyone on Earth was only six acquaintances away from knowing Kevin Bacon, the actor. You once knew someone who knew someone and so on and so on until you found that you were connected to Kevin Bacon after all. A play was written by that name, and then a film. A few years later, Google did an experiment involving over 30 billion emails and other messages. It was found that, actually, 6.6 degrees took in everyone on Earth: Eskimos, nomadic tribesmen and, yes, Neo-Nazis – everyone.

What that seems to tell me is that we are all much more connected than we have dreamed. It also means that it matters how we treat people, even in the most seemingly irrelevant contexts. It matters. Matters a lot.

What it boils down to is this. If you can actually meet someone, shake off the profile you want to hang on them, bite your tongue if necessary, but listen to what they have to say, you are causing a tiny lessening of the centrifugal force that is throwing us into opposing positions. If you can't believe it makes a difference, consider what happens if you do not understand and validate them. Consider where you are sending them into exile, and what response you can expect from them later, when mere conservatives are forced into Neo-Nazi ideology. The goal is not to convince them to join your side; that could be impossible. What you want to accomplish is to reinforce, however briefly, a world you both live in. A place where, despite the divisions, you are together.

Incredible as it seems now, this too shall pass. The return of Trump, the threat of European populism, the folly of Brexit – all these will fade into a history that we cannot now imagine. There will be new threats, new challenges. But how should we best confront them as they come? I think the better angels of our nature come only when they are invited. When we replace dreams of victory with dreams of peace. When we can look at each other – all of us, not just those whose class, race or ideology we cling to – and say, "We are we. The earth on which we plant our feet belongs to, say it: US."

If it doesn't make the world instantly better, don't sweat it. Have you really got anything better to try?

Trust me; I'm only 6.6 degrees away from Mahatma Gandhi.

Up Close and Personal

One day, soon after we arrived in London, my wife, Gilly, and I were on a bus. You're supposed to get on at the front and exit at the back. The bus was crowded, with people standing in the aisles, and we were crawling along through dense traffic in West London. Several people came forward at stops and asked the driver if they could exit from the front door. He obligingly opened the door for them.

At another stop, a woman came forward just like the others. She was a black woman in her forties. The driver was a white man. When she asked him to open the front door, he shook his head. The woman started to plead with him, but he just looked out the windscreen and paid no attention. In the end she had to scramble to the back doors to get off. I saw her walking along the pavement as we crept slowly toward Ealing. She was muttering, and, I believe, cursing. Two streets farther along, she was still there, glaring at the driver and talking to herself.

The incident left me with a sick feeling. It had clearly been a case of discrimination, but the driver hadn't actually done anything improper, according to the rules. But he knew, and she knew, and Gilly and I, sitting embarrassedly near the front, all knew that something ugly had taken place. And it seemed to me, watching the woman's face, that a small homeopathic dose of poison had been released into the flowing current of the city. The waters in which we all swim had become a little darker and, it may be, a little more dangerous.

It reminded me of a story one of the members of the Dublin congregation told me, about a black woman arriving late for a bus, burdened with packages, and holding up the coach's departure by a few minutes. She was politely treated, and when she finally got on board, she was smiling and saying, "I feel blessed. I am blessed."

This corollary, it seems to me is exact: if the woman felt blessed, then the other must have felt cursed. In two routine incidents, repeated millions of times each day, the curse or blessing was released into the world. In each case, they were results that spread beyond the confines of the moment. In the latter, I'm sure everyone aboard the bus felt the warmth of the woman's blessing; on the mean streets of London, I'm sure that others felt the pain of the other woman's curse. These incidents are minor; they don't lend themselves to treatment of law and sanctions. And yet they affect our lives in ways we can't measure. Like the butterfly's wingbeats in the Amazon, they may create a hurricane in Europe.

It isn't a giant leap from that incident to another bus years ago, when a fanatical kid from Leeds blew himself and 14 others up in Tavistock Square. Poison collected over time, nursed in alienation and then carefully cultivated by those who can find a use for it, is ultimately capable of grave acts of violence. Anecdote piled on rumour and cooked in isolation becomes a new and deadly form of abstraction. The years of lynching in my native American South, the so-called "peaceful demonstrations" of the right-wing nationalist groups are examples of this. The banner may read "racial purity" or patriotic fervour. It may also be named "jihad."

Once the anecdotal becomes the abstract, and murder is done under one banner or another, then simple killings become acts of heroism, and mere suicide becomes "martyrdom." It has ceased to be a personal phenomenon at all. That is why I am convinced that people who commit mass murder would probably say, in a chilling echo of the Mafia, "Nothing personal. Just business."

We have all heard of what is called the law of karma. It basically says that all human experience is a result of cause and effect. A parallel to the Newtonian law of physics that states "for every action there is an equal and opposite reaction." The Californian jargon is a bit more understandable: "What goes around comes around."

This is a wise half-truth. I call it a half-truth because it doesn't usually get beyond the concerns of the individual life. At its most basic, it says that if you are violent then you will be the victim of violence. If you are greedy you will be the victim of greed. It is a kind of moral code to keep people in line, a version of the so-called Golden Rule: "Do unto others as you would have them do unto you." In ethical philosophy, it is known as reciprocity. Like any moral prescription, it has its selfish undercurrents. You might as well say, "Be nice to people and you will get a nice reward." That's different from the idea that being nice to people for its own sake is the way to live.

The rabbi Jesus and other masters seem to have had a different take on the subject. When being asked about this odd thing called the "kingdom of heaven", Jesus is reported to have said that it was "at hand." That means *nearby,* by the way; I looked it up. It makes me think that he was saying that the kingdom of heaven was where he was already living, that he was, in fact, the first citizen of a new and different kind of world.

In this world he was living in, things seem irrational. You love your enemies. You bless those who curse you. If someone importunes you for your coat, you give him your shirt as well. If he pops you one, you offer up the other cheek for him to hit. He didn't seem to be saying that this would store up good karma for you, or that, after being hit any number of times that you would, say, win the lottery. He seemed to be saying that the kingdom of heaven works that way. And I get from that that the kingdom of heaven, or the better world we hope for, is acquired just this way – in the foregoing of personal reward for the sake of something much more important. Something frustratingly hard to define, and invisible. By living according to the rules of this kingdom, it seems to say, you are actually helping to bring it about.

But surely we can't actually live as Jesus seemed to be suggesting! We have to look after our own interests. Everything in creation follows that pattern. The lion doesn't avoid eating an impala calf out of pity any more than a big business lion avoids the sad necessity of asset-stripping a small family business. The trees themselves struggle to gain the most light and leave the others in shadow, so of course we compete for jobs and money, sometimes doing things that maybe we shouldn't in order to gain the sunlight of success. It is our biological mandate, that nouveau-Darwinian idea that so excites the prophets of meaninglessness like some of the so-called "new atheists", who are content to identify the selfish gene.

And yet the stories of the great souls are there to disturb our merry competing. The man who sacrifices his life to save a drowning boy. The leader of a liberation struggle making himself a target for assassins. The hedge fund manager, like my friend, a former member at our church in Kensington, who has given over a billion pounds to a charity to help children in Africa. Like sacrificing mothers and grandfathers in all ages, like St Francis of Assisi the leper kisser, and like the unknown millions who have let slide their own advantages in order to bring about something that feels right. So we have this inbuilt value too, and the tug-of-war between the two poles of our natures could be said to define us.

More than anything, I think that is what the tantalising injunctions of the young rabbi Jesus were about. Put simply, if we can learn to hear the far-off anthem of a coming kingdom and let our selfish advantage slip, we may find a way to survive. Maybe not the kingdom of heaven, but certainly a world in which fairness, not transactional morality, sets the agenda.

In very recent times I seem to sense that things have turned a bit uglier. It sometimes seems that there is a kind of tide of goodwill that has surrounded us without our noticing it for most of our years on earth. Not that the harsh realities of the past were not painful and severe, but that there were certain, call them "core values" if you like, that went without analysis because they were always there.

This could be the ranting of a grumpy old man; it wouldn't surprise me if it were. It's not as if teenagers have never gone around stabbing each other. As a recent *Guardian* article pointed out, that's what Romeo and Juliet is all about. It's not as if fanaticism has never before gained the upper hand in political life; there have always been those who were willing to sacrifice their humanity for the sake of an idea. What I am talking about comes in the form of a hunch. I think that a kind of chaos lurks just outside the periphery of our normal lives.

It probably has a lot to do with the gradual working through into everyday perception of the relativity factor unleashed by Einstein and other geniuses. There is no absolute to which we can now cling. Instead of moral certainty, we have the droll slogan of the Beat Generation: "compared to what?" Or as teenagers say it nowadays: "Whatever." We have lost faith, and what is worse, we cannot even imagine how it might be reclaimed. There is no wise God, we fear, who will reward the virtuous and punish the wicked, no court of last resort for the lost and helpless. "In God we trust," emblazoned on every American coin, might well read, "trust the market."

But I think there is something more than the rubbishing of traditional theology at work here. My feeling is that there are things for which we have no name, perhaps things inscribed in our genes that have kept an invisible medium of goodwill within reach. These are root ideas and feelings, so deep that they could hardly even be observed, that made up the field in which we humans have our being. Some things simply are not done. Some things are sacred. Some things will cause pain in the shrivelled conscience of a sociopath. These are the ideas that seem now to be at risk.

People often ask, I do myself, what a purely individual act has to do with the greater sum of human experience. I was nearly stung by a wasp on a train one day not long ago. I flung the insect to the floor and was about to crush him when a man who looked as if he had been sleeping rough put his hand on my arm and said, 'Don't kill him.' It brought me back to myself, and I was grateful. He was exhibiting one of these mysterious hidden ideas that bind us together.

I believe that this tide that can sustain us or wash us away lives in the micro-world of everyday behaviour. That is solely and exclusively where it has its existence. No laws, government programmes, miracle insights can help this. Every one of us, in a very real sense, is responsible for the well-being of the world. That's what the young rabbi was talking about 2,000 years ago. If we can find a way to bless when everything screams at us to curse, we are moving partway into his invisible kingdom. If we can swallow our bile and frustration by acquitting an individual person of another race, an immigrant, a political opponent, a prostitute, from disdain for the whole of their class, we are slopping a little mortar onto a new set of foundations. The foundations of someplace where we all can live.

All of us.

Send in the Clowns

Every once in a while, without knowing why, it seems that something I say from the pulpit is especially meaningful to people sitting out there. If I knew how or why, I wouldn't turn into a grouchy, self-obsessed monster every Thursday, when the need to produce some words and music for the service starts getting urgent. If I knew why, I'd just reel it off, crowd surf out of the room and never give it a single one of my 5 am worry sessions.

The sermons I think are pure dynamite wind up damply squibbing. The longer I practise the disappearing art of sermonising, the less I know about it. I could use another 20 years' practice or so, but that seems unlikely. So I've reached a conclusion: the sermons that move you don't come from me at all; they come from you.

A woman I didn't recognise once approached me after a meeting and said that a sermon she heard me preach had changed her life. Now that's quite a compliment and being as hungry for praise as the next egotist, I asked her which one she meant. She said, 'The story of the sad circus clown.' Of course, I have never preached about a sad circus clown, and I'm giving you a money-back guarantee that I never, ever, will.

What's important is that she *heard* about a clown. That somewhere in her unconscious lived this image that carried meaning for her, and that invoking that may indeed have changed the way she looks at life. I don't begrudge her her sad circus clown, not at all. I wish I could always find everyone's sad circus clown. That symbol of truth belonged to her, and all I did was prompt it, with no more intention than that of a bee looking for honey that winds up fertilising a flower.

What that leads me to believe is that truth is something that cannot be told, not in words, anyway. Maybe it can be conveyed in something as simple as a smile. It seems that truth is already in us, somewhere down below the water line, and that sometimes a line dropped in exactly the right place at exactly the right moment can tap into it. That's what happened with the circus clown lady, and that's what happens when you walk away from hearing a preacher seeming to tell the truth.

Now, get ready. I never thought I'd find myself quoting Donald Rumsfeld. Yes, secretary of so-called defence under both Reagan and George W Bush. I am going to quote him. If you object, please just turn the page. He was one of the planners of the Iraq war, who endorsed such things as "extraordinary rendition" and radical interrogation techniques such as "water-boarding." Not a guy I'd like to get trapped in a lift with.

Rumsfeld is also famous for some lines he spoke in some testimony before a Senate inquiry that, almost unintentionally, shed some light on what we would have to call epistemology. In English as we know it, that means a theory of knowledge. I'll give you the version that comes from Wikipedia, edited just a wee bit:

There are known knowns, things we know and know that we know them. There are known unknowns, things we know that we do not know. And there are also unknown unknowns, things that we don't know and don't know that we don't know them.

He was speaking about Al Qaeda, the missing weapons of mass destruction it was claimed that Saddam had in his armoury, and the terrorist plots that were being hatched virtually everywhere. But he could have been talking about almost anything in life. Without meaning to, he gave an almost complete framework for all knowledge. You can apply it to your own experience.

One *known known*, for instance, is that the Earth revolves around the Sun. You can prove that. It's so. No point arguing about it. Done and dusted. One *known unknown* is about the atmosphere on what they call "Goldilocks planets", distant planets that are capable of supporting Earth-type life. We know that we don't know it yet, but we're working on it. Working on it and feeling confident that one day we will know.

That brings us to Rumsfeld's third category: *unknown unknowns*. It seems to me that these are of two types. Take the asteroid that smacked into a Russian town one year. We didn't know that the object, the size of an Olympic swimming pool, was even there. We only found out about it after the event, when it started some fires and became, in a second, a *known known.* We even have a Wikipedia entry for the Chelyabinsk meteor, as it is now called. That was one kind of *unknown unknown:* things that haven't happened yet.

Another kind of *unknown unknown* can't be described today because we don't even have a category for it. There will be announcements about it someday, perhaps. A new discovery of something that we hadn't even suspected could exist. We'll see it on BBC news at six. Until then, we will just have to leave it out there, not even knowing what to look for.

I said that Rumsfeld almost covered the ground with his categories. Almost, because I believe that there is another category he left out. I'll give it to you in the same convoluted language he used: there are also *unknown knowns.*

If you think that's silly, I don't blame you. Rumsfeld's use of the English language was heavily criticised after his speech. It was said that he was torturing the syntax, and that usages like "known unknowns" would earn a failing grade on an exam paper. I fear it might have been boring or confusing to listen to, so I apologise. I'll just make it worse now, and repeat: I believe that there are *unknown knowns.* Things that we really know, but don't know that we know them.

What I mean by that goes back to what I was saying about the limitations of the human mind. I said that God, the Universe and all that could not be grasped by the mind. You might ask me this: then what tool do we possess that is able to grasp the Big Truth?

Enter the sad circus clown.

If there is any point to religious activity at all, and who hasn't wondered about that, a clue is in the Latin root of the word itself. It's from "re", meaning again, and *"ligare",* to tie or connect. What people who practise it are trying to do is reconnect with a truth that is in us, or of which we are a part. It isn't like philosophy, which seeks to understand things, nor like pure science, which attempts to describe things. It's an attempt to find a connection, a personal link, to the big picture: life, the universe and everything.

There's a story about God sitting around with a few angels, resting from the six days of creation. One of them asks the boss, "Where are you going to stick the truth?" Suggestions emerge: in outer space. "Nope," says God, "I made them clever; they'll get up there someday." "What about deep in the sea?" asks another. "Same problem," says God, "they'll invent something and dive down there too." Finally, an angel whispers in God's big old ear and God shouts, "Great idea! Someplace where it's really hard to go: within their own hearts."

Hidden in the folds of your heart, or, if you prefer, the depths of your soul, is the answer you have taken birth to find. As near as the neck of your camel, as Mohammed said, but almost impossibly difficult to see. When someone does catch a glimpse of it, we call them a mystic or a saint. We might even start a religion on the basis of it. Or, more likely, we might call them mad and feed them pills.

And yet, it is never very far at all from our straining eyes. We look here, we look there, we weigh and measure and give names to everything, set up institutions and make the shelves groan with heady tomes, but don't get it. Even when we sometimes glimpse it in a sunset, a snatch of music or, yes, the smile of a stranger, we don't credit it for what it really is. It's the sad circus clown that tells us: this is the category Rumsfeld left out. This is an *unknown known.* Basic equipment in the human being. The ability to know something without having it reach the level of full awareness.

I start with the idea that we human beings are all equipped with everything we need to do this thing called life. We're not all smart, or pretty, we're not even all physically able. The breaks we get, where we're born, our skin colour, our ability to carry a tune, are not equally distributed. But I believe they're all sufficient for the real task of living: coming to know who you really are.

The thing that makes this possible is the fourth category: the *unknown knowns* Rumsfeld left out. That thing that was tucked into our deep parts at or before birth, which makes all the difference. That means that our task, especially the task of people like us, who are impelled by a hunch to read books like this, is to reconnect with our true origin and our final destiny.

If we hear something that urges us on or touches us deeply, we need to see it not as an accident, but as a road marker. If it takes a sad circus clown to point us in the right direction, then that will do fine. If something in someone touches something in you – well, isn't that the point?

Send in the clowns.

Passing Through

Do you like road movies? That's the new name for what are called picaresque stories, a series of adventures that seem like a random collection of events that somehow add up to a satisfying whole.

I love them, and so does everyone, it seems. Two new ones were recently nominated for Oscars, and won some, too. I think that's because we all have our own road movies, and our own stories to share. And sometimes these stories, coming as they do at just the right moment, make all the difference.

Some years ago now, I had just come back from my second assignment in what we sometimes call the Third World. I stayed a few weeks at Woodbrooke, the Quaker study centre in Birmingham. I had been mostly working with religious groups overseas, though the work was practical and developmental, not theological. Even so, I had suffered the return of an old itch. I like the word itch better than "vocation" or "calling."

Some things had happened to me that had brought up feelings from my childhood, when I had been frogmarched to church every Sunday. Even though I had long ago abandoned any idea of being a conventional Christian, my strange soul now longed to be a minister. Don't ask me to explain that, unless you happen to be a psychiatrist.

While at Woodbrooke I had several tutorials with my old friend John Punshon, who was director of Quaker Studies. One afternoon I told him that I wanted to be a minister. Being a wise man, John told me to just sit on it for a while and see if it went away. I think this is called "testing one's vocation." So I did. A long time later, after another job in Africa, I went to see him again and told him that the itch was getting stronger. He reminded me that I was probably onto a loser. For one thing, Quakers don't even have a professional clergy, so career prospects in that denomination were, to say the least, limited.

One day I saw him in the dining hall, and he asked me to sit next to him. He said, 'Did you ever hear of so-and-so?' (A name I can't remember now, so I'll call him Fred.) I said no. John told me that I should have. He said that he and Fred were very good friends, and he had an interesting story. Knowing that I had been in San Francisco during the so-called Summer of Love, he said that I might have met Fred there, since he was also an ageing hippie. I tried to take that as a compliment.

One day Fred was in his psychedelic flat when there was a knock on the door. He opened it to find a middle-aged man in a Stetson hat and cowboy boots, who immediately asked if Fred knew Jesus. Fred, taken aback, said he had no time for all that. The cowboy just smiled. 'He knows you,' he said.

Fred got involved in an argument at this point. The two sat on the floor and had a philosophical punch-up that went on all afternoon and into the evening. At one point the cowboy pulled a Bible from his hip pocket and started quoting scripture. Fred just about kept up. When the cowboy left, Fred was no closer to being a Christian, but he had discovered an interest in theology and philosophy. The next autumn, he enrolled in a local university and later went back east to Earlham College and got a master's degree in theology.

John told me all this with a smile on his face. He stopped and asked slyly, 'Do you know what Fred does now?' I said I didn't. 'Now he's the clerk of Philadelphia Yearly Meeting!' he said triumphantly. That is, so to speak, the head Quaker in North America.

'But, John,' I said, 'I don't want to be clerk of Philadelphia Yearly Meeting. I just want to be a minister.'

'No, no. You missed the point,' John said, heaving with laughter. 'You can be the cowboy!'

The cowboy, unlike Fred, didn't have a name that we can look up. He was what we would call a mendicant, a traveller. Like many influences in our lives, he was just passing through when he ran into Fred. Whatever his theology consisted of, he is in the company of a lot of great travellers, people like the Buddha, Rumi, Milarepa, Lao Tse and even Jesus. His job was to meet people, and using no tool greater than his own experience, influence the outcome of their lives.

A lot of the important meetings in my own life have been fleeting. I spent a drunken evening with the hero of my adolescence, Jack Kerouac –

the original On the Road himself. Someday, if you promise not to tell, I'll give you the whole story, one that changed the way I look at things forever. All I'll say now is that I put my thumb out and hitchhiked from Jacksonville, Florida to San Francisco on the back of it. That might be someone you have heard of, but there have been many more who are not famous. Each one of these meetings has done something to me. If you look at your own experience, you will recognise the same sort of thing.

It's very noticeable that most of the things we respect in our culture are things connected with permanence. We like established histories. If you look at plaques on the walls of churches, you will find that the most revered figures are the ones with the most longevity. We equate staying power with authority. We tend not to like the temporary, and so do what we can to make things last. When things ultimately do pass away, we erect monuments. Just have a look at the gilded lily in Kensington Gardens erected by Queen Victoria for her dead husband or take a trip to the marble halls of the Taj Mahal. As for church architecture, we build giant heaps of carved stone in memory of someone whose ministry lasted three years and who, unlike the foxes and birds, had no home at all.

We shouldn't blame ourselves for this obsession with the lasting. It speaks of that uniquely human gift, self-awareness and the knowledge of death. From the first stone circles to the latest cathedral spires, we are defiantly trying to stake a claim for the permanence of our lives in a fading universe. But it's all an illusion, of course. St Paul's is literally melting in the rain, and the Parthenon is being eaten away by exhaust fumes. Photographs taken in hopes of celluloid immortality wind up in landfill sites.

We make much of old relationships, too. That is what the scourge of nationalism is all about. That's why gypsies have always been suspect and sometimes treated with genocide. Wandering people disturb us, and their expulsion or extinction helps with our game of denial. We overlook the fact that the roaming Troubadours served as the wake-up call for the dark ages. That heroes like the Buddha were travellers. That language and culture in West Africa were spread by nomadic tribespeople.

We forget the mounds of soulful literature in which all spiritual life is described as a journey and dismiss as quaint the plaintive tones of African slave music; "Ain't got no home in this world, Lord."

Leaving one's country of birth is always like that. You may have great reasons for changing nationality, and you may embrace the new land with what feels like total enthusiasm. But then, one day, you'll catch a glimpse of a landscape that reminds you of your former home and get floored by a wave of nostalgia. In my case, I was watching the Masters golf competition on television one day when I heard a train whistle in the background. It was a long, plaintive, gooseflesh-raising sound I heard constantly as a kid, but never took particular notice of. It went directly to my heart and set off a tide of reflection that hasn't ended yet.

It seems that though our minds want to glue themselves to permanence, our souls actually may be quietly content with change. From time to time they give us a little reminder, that permanence, lovely as it seems, just isn't available here. So that makes me think that we ought to try to make a few changes in the way we look at things.

It tells me that any moment is an opportunity for life-changing experience. The person sitting next to you on a train may not be a Zen master, but you'd better be prepared in case he is. And bad news has a way of turning out to be a blessing. We know that from stories. We know that, but perhaps wary of clichés, pretend we don't. Every meeting with a loved one might be the last, so that helps centre you in moments of discord. It can take the edge off personal ambition, too, if you realise that the edifice you are building is just waiting for the wrecking ball. You can be the most loyal of servants, make your forty years, get a gold watch and everything, and then be forgotten like last Tuesday's dinner.

We are all just passing through. We are, as the Youngbloods sang, echoing Francis Thompson, "a moment's sunlight, fading on the grass." Knowing that, taking it fully on board, we can embrace the mendicant life. Instead of clinging to worn-out relationships, we can learn to love the slap of our sandals on the roads. Instead of clinging to achievement and honour, we can discard them the way we do recrimination and blame.

This business of passing through, it seems to me, is what spiritual growth is all about. The "chance" encounter with someone, a few fleeting moments of intensity with a stranger, the glimpse of paradise in some landscape from a train window: all of these things do more of the work of revealing the holy than theological colleges and all the philosophical concepts in the world. The effect these things have on your soul may pass by unnoticed but may change you forever. And that means the effect you have on other people's lives may pass equally unnoticed by you but change them forever, too.

It's no accident that stories of the road are the stuff of our most engrossing literature. They are the stuff of our own inner journeys toward becoming who we really are. Our own *Canterbury Tales, Don Quixote, Pilgrim's Progress* and raft voyage down the Mississippi with Huck Finn. Passing through is more than drifting; it is a purposeful trip toward a goal we can hardly remember, pages turned in a divine romance we will one day read, and understand.

Who are you sitting next to, on the train or in church? What do they have to tell you that will change your life? Are you listening?

What, Me Worry?

What are you worried about today?

If you can't answer right away because you're feeling pretty good at the moment, I can help you out by giving you a small list of things to worry about. I've recently been writing a book with a friend of mine and between us we have become pretty expert at finding scary things we'd rather not think about. Things like the asteroid Apophys, which is coming perilously near Earth's orbit not too far in the future. Or the great volcano in Wyoming that could basically end the world in a few weeks' time and is now 40,000 years overdue.

What about the recent solar flares we have been experiencing, scheduled to get much worse over the next few years, and having the power to completely eliminate digital technology? Or about the big chunk of mountain hanging perilously off the edge of one of the Canary Islands, which might well cause devastating tsunamis like the modern world has never seen?

No? Well, there's the new organism recently discovered in India that has the unique ability to make every strain of bacteria on earth immune to antibiotics. And the leakage of industrial materials that imitate the effects of oestrogen that are threatening to destroy the world's coral reefs and with them half of the fish crop.

None of these things are made up; you can see them all in the pages of your daily newspaper. If you began to obsess about any of them you would wind up suicidally depressed or alcohol dependent, at least. Our lives are chock-a-block with things we choose not to think about. We push them out of our minds into a cellar that we long ago dedicated as a kind of glory hole for the unthinkable. Some people refer to this cellar as the unconscious. It's full of stuff we can't or won't look at, and we kid ourselves that if we don't think about them, they will just go away.

But there are other events that loom in our personal lives, aren't there? One day each of us will die. Even our children will not always be peachy and smooth; they will grow old, lose their hair and their hearing, and even they will die. There is a whole compendium of possible doomsday scenarios that might occur. Not *might,* will.

There are times when you wake early and lie in bed and all the horrors come at you at once. Some vision of the world so bleak that it chills your heart and shakes your bones. It happened to me just the other day. In those times you might pray if you are able. You might revert to some magic formula of childhood, when there were witches in the wardrobe, and you had a secret charm to ward them off. More likely, you will find some way to distract yourself, with a favourite addiction or rationalisation. If you are lucky, the moment will pass. The demons go back into the basement for a time. Things seem okay.

Even though the demons seem to leave you alone, they don't really disappear. Because the work of ignoring them can sap your energy and make you lose out on life. And we have strong hints that behind the curtain of fear and anxiety lies a wealth of undiscovered gifts.

When there are un-faced fears and unmet challenges in our lives, the will to growth will find a way to reveal them. That's not speculation, you know; that's a fact. Even if we can avoid confrontation with our nightmares for decades, there is a price to pay. We might get sick. We might be unable to settle in relationships. We might even go mad.

All of the great teachers tell us that we need to abandon the clinging grip of the past and the bracing against the future and get involved in what is sometimes called the Eternal Now. It was Jesus who said, "Sufficient unto the day are the evils thereof ... take no thought for the morrow." Buddha practised the awareness of the present, as has Zen technique ever since. The Sufis view the present as the point where time and eternity merge. Gestalt technique is about delivering the psyche from past longings and future anticipations, by, as Ram Dass always says, "Being here now."

But being in the present, the Eternal Now, doesn't just involve conscious abandonment of past and future. It also means leaving behind those attachments and anxieties that we are unaware of, that is, all that stuff in the cellar. If you're braced against thinking the unthinkable all the time, you live not in the active present, but in a shadowy fortress that is neither present nor future. The appreciation of the Now is made impossible by the effort of evading the acknowledgement of grim future realities and the soul-robbing influence of unresolved guilt. If the witch is in the wardrobe, we will only lose by trying with all our strength to ignore her. Much better to call her out, warts and all, and see if we can learn from her.

A few years ago, I learned a certain technique from a therapist I was seeing. I love techniques because they are practical; all that philosophy is fine and inspiring but, in the immortal words of Paul Simon, the real question is: "Breakdowns come and breakdowns go. Whatcha gonna do about it; that's what I'd like to know."

My therapist told me that we all have something called "the myth that I can't bear it." She said that when depression and anxiety set in, just like on one of those bleak mornings, we need to welcome it as an opportunity to learn and grow. If we confront the frightful images as they start picking at the seams of our minds, we might discover not a demon, but a friend. She said that when you allow your terrors to coalesce and take shape, you should then set about eliminating the myth of not being able to bear it. She told me to bear it for thirty seconds, to really let it get hold of me, and just go with the image. After as much as you can stand, you release it, perform whatever acts of personal magic you use: denial, addiction, sublimation, distraction, making a nice cup of tea, whatever. And the next time you do that again. In my experience, you not only find that you can bear it all, but that the worst thing about it all along was the fear, not the reality.

Fear, as many have realised, is the opposite of love. When you fear something, your first instinct is to flee. When we live ruled by fear, or its lesser relative, anxiety, loving becomes difficult or impossible. Relationships become guarded. Self-revelation, which is the truest gift you can offer, becomes unlikely. And just as fear opposes love, worry opposes happiness. One cancels out the other.

The teacher Meher Baba was frustrating to his many devotees. Not only did he maintain physical silence, he could be very sparing of advice, as well. People who were drawn to him used to ask for some techniques, some iron-clad methods for spiritually advancing. But Baba would indicate that the path of each was an individual one, and that no one set of guidelines worked for everyone.

One thing he did say, though, later became the name of a popular calypso song. He said, "Don't worry. Be happy." Some people thought this was just an amusing and anodyne little slogan when he gave it to his adherents. But Baba was adamant; he said that it was the way, the only way, to approach the threshold of God. He said that when you worry, you are entering the zone of fear. Fear is the opposite of love. Fear is the sentry post of the small ego self. In fear, you wall yourself off from life, curl up your toes and check your breath. Not so with love, when you can manage to stay there. It is only in openness to life through love that truth is apprehended. He saw it as a kind of rule; not worrying and being happy is the act of trusting in God, not avoiding Him or Her. Tantalisingly, he also said, "God can't do His work with you if you are afraid."

Hippies from my generation over-used and misused a common word: paranoia. This word from the tomes of psychoanalysis springs from the Greek for "madness" and generally referred to people who were delusional. Typically, this would mean a sense of persecution coupled with an exaggerated idea of one's importance. In common speech, however, it was used to indicate any feeling of anxiety.

But if you think about it, it seems to become more relevant after all. The small self, trying to protect itself with a bundle of personal magic charms, things like public honours, solid financial net worth, a large Christmas card list, can feel threatened by such natural things as ageing, one's share of bad luck in investments, and occasional bad health. The fact that these things happen to everyone doesn't seem to apply. Not when they are happening to precious, special, irreplaceable ME.

Someone really gripped by fear and the defence mechanisms arrayed for self-protection cannot be a loving person. There's just no psychic space left to admit anyone else.

I'll offer you another Greek word from the same root. This one is *metanoia.* It's so infrequently used that the spell checker on my computer is stumped when I write it down. The closest match it can offer is "melanoma". A pity, because what it means is a change of mind, or heart, what you might call a conversion experience.

It has been used by Christians for their brand of conversion, like Paul's on the road to Damascus. It means a kind of rewiring of the attitude, in which those tight bonds that have held you in a static grip loosen enough to let you imagine yourself and others in a different way. What has seemed threatening can become friendly, even wonderful. What has been frightening can become enlightening, as when Paul realised that the itinerant preacher Jesus wasn't persecuting him with his non-traditional Jewish teachings; it was Paul who was the persecutor.

But this is not an invitation to become a born-again believer. For my money, Paul seemed to lapse into a form of paranoia later into his mission, when he was trying to control a ragged band of believers around the Mediterranean. It is an invitation, not just to you, but to me. The invitation is to stop running from what scares us, to stop building high walls of rationalisation and defence around ourselves. That's no way to live. One cliché about Unitarians is that we don't worry about life after death; we prefer life before death.

Metanoia most often comes as the result of a crisis. But I believe there's no reason to wait for an occasion when we have no option but to accept reality. I think it's possible to go out there and deal with the things that frighten us, knowing that apparent safety is no bargain. The price we pay for it is just too high. What it is costing us is the ability to live.

When Roosevelt said that the only thing we have to fear is fear itself, he wasn't just referring to the panic in the stock market. Maybe he knew that, and maybe he didn't, but we have an opportunity to grasp it at the root. When we stop fearing, we start loving. And when we start loving, the truth that makes us really safe is clearly seen.

So, what are you worried about today?

Welcome to Fort Attitude

Did anyone besides me ever see *The Dog Whisperer* on television? It featured a dog trainer named Cesar Millan, who has an uncanny grasp of what animals experience. So much so that he can tame a snarling, dangerous pit bull terrier in a matter of a few minutes. He does this with what I understand to be some of the techniques of Gestalt psychology, in which whatever is happening in the active present is all one needs to deal with almost any situation. I admire him and have learned a few things that have become useful in other areas of my life. Yes, including ministry.

One of the things Cesar focuses on is what we would call "attitude". Dogs are expert at reading the mood states and intentions of the people who handle them. The wrong attitude creates the wrong result, no matter how rigorous the training methods are.

Now "attitude" is a neutral word if you look it up in the dictionary. You can have a positive or negative one. It's as empty of content as the word "quality". But, just like quality, attitude now means something else. It has become a kind of slang or slogan word for a state of mind that is belligerent or quarrelsome or unpleasant in some other way. "The guy's got attitude," you might hear someone say. Maybe especially if he or she is American, since the people of my homeland seem to make a deliberate effort to mangle the Queen's English at every turn. Maybe just to annoy British people.

We all know people with attitude. You know, the types who always have to be accommodated in conversation, because you know that they are guarding something. I have heard it said about a person that "You can feel his attitude coming before he walks into the room." There are those whose own unfulfilled psychological needs bring attitude-laden tension into ordinary conversation. The badly parented adult, nursing a need to be stroked or punished, for example. The disappointed older gent who sees nearly everything as a sign that the world is going to hell in a hand basket. The bitter animal-rightster, feminist or nationalist, also.

Not that all these positions aren't okay in their own right, but that they're frequently accompanied by a prickly and defensive attitude. There are people around whom you would never mention anything to do with politics, because you never know when you will be uncorking a gust of opinion. As a member of the church told me recently, 'You men have been made nervous about saying some things in case it offends women.' Too much so, she meant. I took that as a kindness, but God help the man who uses phrases like "the man in the street" or even the pronoun "he" when it could equally be "she". I bless those female friends of mine who don't bristle when someone inadvertently says "lady" instead of "woman". I'd blow you all a kiss if that wasn't sexist too.

Well, here's the bad news: we all have attitude. True enough, if we surround ourselves with people whose attitude problems match our own it's possible not to notice much. We probably share a lot of attitudes; it isn't too difficult talking about, say, the Iraq war. You can be pretty sure that you won't offend others if you are liberal about sexuality. It's when things get a little closer to home that we run into our own untamed pit bulls. That may be why we keep things light except with our closest friends and colleagues, whose collaboration in our issues has been worked out over time, and in whose presence we have, in turn, learned to move carefully.

When something happens to expose our attitudes, though, there is a wealth of learning available to us if we have the good sense and the stomach to pay attention. Ask any good psychotherapist; if you probe for sensitive spots in a person's self-presentation, you strike gold. If the mention of motherhood, say, creates a noticeably defensive or scratchy reaction in a client, bingo! You have hit pay dirt. That's where you need to start digging, but very, very carefully. The spiky parts of people's attitudes are like loose threads hanging off a sweater; pull one and the whole garment will unravel. You could say that attitude is the x that marks the spot on a psychological treasure map.

Most of us arrange to keep our attitudes intact by a series of unconscious ruses. But sometimes something happens that uncovers them without our consent. A slip of the tongue in a key moment, perhaps. Or being thrust into a new situation where the rules of survival aren't yet clear. Remember the aftermath of Hurricane Katrina in the Gulf states of the US? The event threw up a veritable avalanche of attitude. Depending on who you talked to, you could hear that God sent the storm to punish the evils of gambling and sinful carousal in the French Quarter and the casinos of Biloxi. Environmentalists queued up to say that it was all down to global warming ultimately brought about by the burning of all that oil that is sucked from the Gulf seabed. Others, who opposed the Iraq war, pointed out that the levees and coastal defenses were left unrepaired because of funds spent in Iraq.

The attitude of others is more easily spotted, however, than our own. From our earliest thinking days, we begin to accumulate it. Some of it comes from our parents and siblings, and our backgrounds at school. By the time we are teenagers we have become avid collectors of attitude. Just ask your favourite teenager what he or she thinks about something topical. The answer you get will usually be couched in extremes: "I can't stand her!" "Ooh, she's *wonderful!*" Not much room there for moderation. If you do get what sounds like a moderate opinion, "Oh, he's all right," you can bet that the matter doesn't touch the life of the teenager in any way.

What we are doing at that age is building our own small castles. The bricks are the carefully cultivated opinions, weighed in the balances of burgeoning social status and added to the totality of our "personalities". From the castle tower we will be able to survey the world in relation to its threat or advantage to our positions. Behind its walls we feel secure and at home. The others who have been permitted inside are allies, and those outside are strangers (stroke) enemies. The only problem that we may have is the old-fashioned one of siege; even the most strongly defended fortress must rely on fresh supplies from outside.

If you think this metaphor applies only to adolescents, though, think again. If it seems obvious that it applies to members of the BNP, say, or a radical loyalist cell on the other island, but not to the person next to you on the pew, I'm sorry to have to say that we are all peering at each other from the castellated walls of our own opinion castles. Everybody is lord or lady of all they survey and prisoner in the dungeon at the same time. Fort Attitude – that's what we ought to call it.

All those lovely opinions we were so proud of! The ones that set us apart from the others and made us strong and viable in our limited little ego life. I recently offended a friend of mine. He is a *Daily Telegraph* reader and a true-blue Tory, but we have worked out ways of relating that turned the differences of opinion into a sort of game, with laughter on both sides. But during an election, he sent me an email calling the Labour Party something like a "stable full of braying jackasses". I agreed that they weren't exactly thrilling me either, but said, 'Surely you can't believe that those overfed and over-coiffed old boys from Eton have your best interests at heart?' I got back an email that was near to smoking with intensity. Our attitudes hadn't seemed so funny after years of separation. I don't know what we'll do about our relationship in the future.

But surely, you say, surely you can't mean that all opinions are wrong. What about principles? About morality? About ... er ... theology? Aren't our carefully derived ideas an essential part of who we are? And if you tried to live without an inner structure of ideas, a personal philosophy, wouldn't you become no better than an animal?

The short answer is only half serious: I wouldn't mind being more like, say, a golden retriever. But the long answer is that if I want to see clearly, I have got to get out of the castle, across the moat, and into the world. That doesn't mean abandoning ideas and ideals; it means turning them from hard bricks back into the malleable clay from which they were made. It means approaching situations with more openness than guardedness. It means that instead of using previously formed beliefs to pass or fail something that I come across, using them as ingredients in a new, less impermeable vision of the world. It means making moral decisions of all kinds on the merits of unique individual situations, not by consulting an inner checklist of pre-digested criteria.

But we can't just leave the matter there. We need to turn this idea inward. Are we to abandon our opinions? Is that what we must do to be saved?

For that, we have to go to the specialists. People like Jesus, who said that to get into the kingdom of heaven, you had to be like a little child. I take that to mean "attitude-free". To the great spiritual master Meher Baba, who, by way of demonstrating the uselessness of mere words, maintained complete physical silence for 43 years. It was he who said those words I use so often: "Trying to understand God is like trying to see with your ears." Meaning that your ideas about God are not God. The Dalai Lama, who often says he possesses no special spiritual consciousness, who is as likely to listen with complete lack of defensiveness to a white supremacist as to a Buddhist monk and then smile and tell them both the same thing: "Just be kind."

Have you ever had a very strong personal experience of something genuinely transcendent? Yes, I am probably talking about what is called a mystical experience. If you have, you will recognise what I'm going to say about it. It seems to happen like this: the rush of words through your brain, the floods of ideas and opinions, in fact, all your attitude, seem in that instant to disappear. Whatever bright gems of reason and opinion you may have brought to the moment just appear to fade. Values and standards melt like dewdrops on the car bonnet. Plans and projects fall away. And all your ideas seem to fall short, because *believing* isn't a match for *knowing.* And theology can't hold a candle to that reality.

I find that during that moment, you couldn't muster an attitude if your life depended on it. In this state of grace you find that you cannot predict or prevent, control or consecrate, but only participate in that completeness that lies beyond opinion. And that all you really want to do is tell someone how grateful you are. That someone might be sometimes called God, since there isn't really anybody else around. And so what you say turns out to be prayer.

That's the swap I'd make in a New York minute: attitude for gratitude. Experiencing reality instead of theorising about it. I'd trade my pit bull in forever, if I could. And maybe someday I will. Maybe someday we all will.

Seeing in the Dark

I spent a year of my younger life in a poor mountain village called Rio Limpio in the Dominican Republic near the border with Haiti. My wife and I inhabited a palm board shack nine feet by fifteen, with a palm-thatched roof.

The agency that sent us there had a rather hair-shirt view of how volunteers should live. So, we had no car, no access to telephones, no electricity or running water. The nearest point of what we might think of as civilisation was fifteen miles away, an army post with a radio. There were no cars at all in the village.

Epifanio was a dry land rice farmer. He lived in a pine board shack across the ditch from me. He had five children, but only one son, a six-year-old named Diogenes, who had a headful of dreadlocks. Epifanio was something of a con man. He befriended me as soon as I arrived in the village, and whether I wanted it or not, he became a frequent visitor. My wife and I had the only bottled gas cooker in the village, and he would sometimes come around and ask to watch us boil water on it. He coveted it as much as any child does a video game, and watched it as obsessively, grinning when our tea kettle whistled.

I learned that Epifanio had once been a great singer. He led the *coplas*, rhyming choruses, at parties, and had been asked by the visiting priest to sing at mass. He had a stringless guitar hanging on the wall over his bed, but he never let anyone take it down. One day, I asked him about this. He said that his wife, Blanquita, had given birth to three boys before Diogenes was born, but that all had died in infancy, the oldest at five. They died of ordinary diarrhoea. When Diogenes came along, the last of his children, he had made a pact with God. If God spared his son's life, he would do two things: he would give up singing, the thing he loved most, and he wouldn't cut Diogenes' hair until he was twelve years old. Knowing Epifanio, I was fairly sure that he had also made a deal with some of the older gods, the

African ones that lived behind the altar. These were people of African descent with close connections to voodoo and the spirit world.

Rio Limpio was a poor village created as a colony by the dictator Trujillo in the 1920s. He wanted these *colonias* to serve as a "living fence" against the encroachment of the even more desperately poor Haitians. Everybody in the village had a little land when the *colonia* started, but gradually, as these things go, a few got relatively richer and some became completely landless. Epifanio's father had been one of the poor ones. It had made Epifanio sly, and therefore, not dead. He had a pair of Wellington boots cadged off some Peace Corps volunteer, and a pair of leather shoes he kept well-polished but never wore. Sometimes he would get a little money from God knows where. He would convince a passing truck driver to buy and bring back a pig from the market fifty miles away. He would blow a conch shell horn at six in the morning, and when the queue formed, he would slaughter the pig and sell all its meat in two hours, doubling his money. Then he'd get drunk for a few days and gamble on the radio lottery everybody in Latin America plays: the quiniela.

Epifanio's nephew, Ramon, used to bring us our water. This was muddy, straight from the river below. The locals drank it as it was. We used to filter and boil it on our gas cooker, something that amazed everyone. I was evangelistic. Didn't people know that if you boil your water your kids wouldn't get diarrhoea? That was before I realised that every child in the village spent hours trekking to the diminishing woodlands, several miles away, to haul firewood. Boiling water takes a lot of wood. And one of the reasons I was there was to help prevent deforestation.

When you fly over the island of Hispanola, you can tell where the DR ends and Haiti begins, because on the Haitian side there are no trees. No trees means less rainfall. It also means terrible erosion of topsoil. This means no food. It is the vicious cycle that engulfs several billion people in the world. The government outlaws the cutting of trees, but they can't enforce it, because they have no answer to the question of fuel. It was routine for children as they passed a tree to furtively take a knife and ring the bark all the way around. In a season, the tree would die, and with a little night-time assistance, it would fall. You can cut up all the dead trees you like. Everybody in Rio Limpio was a tree criminal.

When kids get diarrhoea, they often die. More children die from it than any other cause. Even if you have the disease, you can get rehydration medicines and antibiotics and save their lives. That is, if you have a clinic. Rio Limpio had a wonderful new cement block clinic, built by the last government but one. Then the IMF told the Dominican government that they would have to begin an austerity programme, or else they wouldn't be bailed out of a financial crisis. Does that sound familiar?

In Rio Limpio this meant the closing of the clinic. It sat there behind a chain link fence to keep out people who might steal tin roofing and window glass. Once a week a paramedic would come along on a moped. He would sit on the porch of the clinic and read the newspaper. He didn't see patients because he had no equipment or medicines. I talked to him sometimes. If he had a little money, he'd bring some aspirin tablets with him, but nothing for diarrhoea. Nothing for the children.

Epifanio didn't see the connection between deforestation, diarrhoea and the IMF. He was enmeshed in the fabric of Third World poverty that prevents analysis. He couldn't imagine much beyond his next pig and the arrival of Diogenes with the night's firewood. He relied on the black and white gods and never sang. But to my continual amazement, he was one of the most cheerful people I had ever met.

This cheerfulness was so evident with him that I would sometimes begin to smile as soon as I saw him. He couldn't sing, but he could whistle, which he did often. He usually had some sort of wound from the hard graft of hoeing steep hillsides and carrying big stones. Because of that, I never felt I could complain about anything in our rough existence. His jack-o-lantern smile seemed to banish my self-pity.

My wife and I bought packages of electrolyte rehydration formula and penicillin to fight diarrhoea. We worried sometimes that someone might be allergic to it, but that didn't stop us. I bought it with some money I gouged out of students back home through a local appeal. The paramedic gave out some, and we gave out the rest. It was another case of local, limited help for just a few. I wanted to fly to Washington with Diogenes, dreadlocks and all, and march into the offices of the World Bank and knock some heads together. But that's just another crime; there are enough being committed already. What I really wanted was to hear Epifanio sing.

Epifanio did something for me. He taught me how to see in the dark. When we were called upon to walk along the rutted dirt roads of Rio Limpio by night, I always used a small torch to guide my steps. There were steep places, where the unwary could trip on the hardened ruts or go over steep sides of ravines. During a Christmas celebration that went on too late, I was easing my way back to our shack, where my wife, already tired of the seasonal village hilarity, was asleep.

One of the things that it was difficult to come by in such a remote village was batteries. I realised as I set out that the torch light was dimming and about to fail. I was standing trying to coax more life out of the batteries when Epifanio appeared. He asked if I was lost. I said no, that I was blind. I meant that without some form of external illumination, I wouldn't be able to navigate.

'You don't need that thing,' he said. I couldn't see his face, but I knew he was beaming at me with his gap-toothed smile. 'Stand here for a minute and just look.' I did. 'What do you see?' he asked me. 'Not a lot,' I said. 'Keep looking,' was his reply. So I did.

It was like opening your eyes under water. I could feel the air on my eyeballs, but everything was black. Then, as the last scraps of feeble torchlight faded, the first things I saw were stars. The moon was down, but the sky was well lit up with starlight. Next, I saw the horizon of hills at the far side of town. Then objects appeared: houses and fences. After a few moments, I turned and saw Epifanio's face. He was grinning, just as I suspected.

'Now,' he said, 'let's walk.'

So we did. I learned that it was more a matter of interpreting what I could make out in the gloom than being able to examine anything closely. But I could see very faint shadows that marked the ruts in the road, and I could see when the path turned off that led to my house. My wife had left a kerosene lamp burning for me inside the door. I told Epifanio goodnight and went in. In the well-lit room, I felt almost sorry that I could see so easily. I was aware that Epifanio had taught me something, something that I didn't want to lose.

I'm pretty sure Epifanio has never heard of a metaphor. So he would never suspect that he had taught me a secret about life and living as well as how to get home from a party. It also told me why this man was cheerful. It was because he knew how to see in the dark.

We sophisticates can tease out the meaning from that. Epifanio and billions like him live in a kind of darkness imposed upon them from birth. We may ask our children, "What do you want to be when you grow up?" In places like Rio Limpio, the question would be more like "Will you grow up?" There would be no notion of what the child would do, either. Forces beyond their control would see to that.

But life has a way of levelling things out to the liver. In a world without light bulbs and batteries, what do you do? You learn to see in the dark, that's what. Love your kids, feast when you can and whistle when you can't.

Darkness takes lots of forms. We have our own share of it, though it doesn't bear that name. And sometimes, things seem to get very dark indeed. So I think I'll repeat Epifanio's suggestion:

'Open your eyes. What do you see? Let's walk.'

Working without a Net

Do you ever hear songs or phrases that seem to stick with you without any apparent reason? No, I don't mean those awful attacks of songs you don't even like that you can't stop replaying in your head. I sometimes get hymns stuck in there after I've looked around to pick them out. The only remedy is to shuffle the pack by listening to something you DO like, but then you run the risk of wearing it out and not liking it anymore.

What I'm referring to is more about some thread of meaning. Something you may not quite understand but which somehow lodges in your head. One such for me was a song by Waylon Jennings, a singer I don't much like, who did a background piece for the film *The Executioner's Song* back in the 1980s. This movie was about the execution of Gary Gilmore, who broke the log jam of capital punishment suspensions and died by firing squad in Utah.

The film was horrific in any number of ways, and stitched into that bleak scenario were these lines:

We don't even know where we are.
They say that we're circling a star.
Well, I'll take their word – I don't know.
I'm dizzy, so maybe it's so.

In those simple lines, our biggest human mystery was revealed. As a child, I used to love looking up into the stars and getting a sense of the immensity of the universe. But sometime along the way, I'm not sure exactly when, that very immensity began to seem oppressive. And as I learned more of what the super scientists like Brian Cox have to say, that big, interesting universe out there started to seem alien and threatening. It's one thing to sit securely on a fixed bit of immovable earth and wonder about the stars, as the ancients must have done. But it's another thing altogether when you become aware that we too are swirling in vast, empty space, with no up and no down.

In the village in southern Spain where I have a little cottage, the cemetery sits on top of the highest hill. And next to it is a gigantic rock, the size of a freight car, which has been entirely painted white, as it has been for centuries. This is to serve as a marker for Jesus, when he comes to raise the dead from the graves. They are taking no chances that their small village will be overlooked, as it has been by governments of the past. It's not hard to identify with them. In a universe so vast, the small child in each of us might say, "How can I be found?" Even if there is someone or something that will come and collect me, how on earth – or maybe how in space – will they find me?

The sensation of being in space, of weightlessness, is sometimes reported to be one in which you feel that you're falling, which is the only natural way for humans to feel no pull of gravity, at least for the interval between the cliff edge and the ground below. And if there's no real up and no real down, that's not a bad description of what is actually happening.

It can get a bit scary. It seemed to me that the only way out of the problem is simply this: to turn falling into leaping.

The existentialist theologian Soren Kierkegaard talked about something he called the "leap of faith". This was a leap that had to be made by everyone at some point in his or her spiritual lives. After you have read all the books, heard all the sermons and sung all the hymns, there remains this one solitary act. If you have been looking for the proof of God and Heaven, you have struck out. If you had asked the minister, the rabbi or the priest a hundred times for assurance, you have received nothing but opinion. At this point you have a few options. You could go on attending church or synagogue, trying to auto-hypnotise yourself into a sense of security. You could, as so many do, shrug and forget about the whole religion thing until forced to consider it in some future crisis. Or you could listen to Kierkegaard and take the leap of faith.

To make the leap of faith, it is first necessary to find the cliff edge. This isn't something you can do in your spare time. It involves a lot of thrashing about in the undergrowth of life, taking blind alleys and avoiding mirages in deserts. To reach the abyss takes a lot of living. It means being restless within your life, experiencing a feeling of incompleteness with the ordinary rewards of existence, a sense that there is something more than this. Often it will take the form of a life crisis, bereavement, for example. The thing is, all roads lead to the edge if you follow them long enough. There comes a time when it just isn't enough to have gilt-edged stocks and deluxe insurance policies.

The cliff edge may just pop up out of nowhere. It may be composed of the ordinary events of life. It may come at breakfast time, as in the case of W. H. Auden's poem where he says, "The crack in the teacup leads on to the land of the dead." It may come gradually, with aging. It may come as a result of the innocent questions asked by our children. It may be ignored for a time, maybe a long time, but when it appears you realise it has never been far away.

Standing on the cliff means coming to the end of theory and speculation. However lucid your theories of life have been, however firm your grasp of biology and physics, you are faced with the unknown and unknowable. The abyss of uncertainty is there, an undeniable fact. Belief is not very helpful, because you have the uneasy feeling that belief was just an invented creation of the limited mind. What makes pretty conversation in seminars isn't much use at the cliff edge. What you need is that most elusive thing of all: *faith.*

Faith isn't dependent upon theories and doctrine. That is just the wrapping we give it when we organise religions. Faith, we have good reason to think, is a kind of perception, a sensing organ like your nose and ears. Where belief proposes, calculates, speculates, faith *perceives*. A good explanation of this is found in the Book of Hebrews. The writer, until the last century erroneously supposed to be Paul, says: "Faith is the substance of things hoped for, the evidence of things unseen." In other words, faith is not a concept but a perception. With it you have substance and evidence, not wishes and ideas.

Kierkegaard seems to be saying that faith comes only after a leap. You can't have it sitting on the firm ground; it is only available when you launch yourself into space. It isn't a weekend activity at all. There is a kind of lock on the door to faith that goes like this: you can't have it unless you take the risk that you'll find nothing at all. A lovely cosmic joke with an unknown punch line. It's only available when nothing else will do.

The Nigerian writer Ben Okri wrote a book a few years ago called *Astonishing the Gods.* In one chapter he has a character stumbling onto the abyss, an uncrossable chasm. There is only one way across: an invisible bridge. This bridge is composed of mist, of light, of feelings. It can sometimes be glimpsed, but it seems too insubstantial to stand on. Yet that is exactly, we are told, what you must do. This is only possible when there is no other route to take. You have to be desperate to cross the abyss, which means you have to be good and fed up with all the diversions and detours of your personal history. You have to become exhausted with false trails and red herrings. The longing to cross over has to become very great, even greater than your fear. When you glimpse the bridge, you have the opportunity to cross. This might happen many times or only once.

Okri treats us to a vision of what happens to you if you don't cross the bridge, if you bottle out at the crucial moment. He says you will become half-dead, half-alive. Dustmen will collect you and use you as a negative example. These are harsh words, harsher even than the faith-by-gunpoint theology of the fundamentalists, who merely say you'll burn in hell. What Okri is talking about is the soul; the errands of the spiritual path must be met and accomplished, or one has no life at all.

Okri and Kierkegaard both seem to be saying that it is somehow possible to make faith. You have to keep the bridge intact by walking on it. At each step it may seem too insubstantial to bear your weight. With each footstep it may be that your little scheming brain wants to say, "What?" and give up the whole thing. But each stride builds more bridge to step upon; it is the act of walking that creates the struts and girders out of mist.

This is more than challenging. This is the most crucial undertaking of all. We are being asked to take our small store of inspiration and trust and put everything on it. We are asked to do that if we are Christian, Jew, Pagan or agnostic. We have to sift through the words of Jesus, Rumi and Marcus Aurelius and the observations from our own lives and cobble together a bridge-building kit. And we have to do it with no guarantees. None whatever, except for the inner whisper that grows louder as we get closer to the void. That still small voice has to grow until it overwhelms the great roar of conversation that is our individual psyche.

I believe that, as Hafiz said, "When the rider is ready, the horse appears." What we will need to cross the chasm is already there within us. It needs to become ready for use, and that is what the ups and downs of life are for. When we finally launch ourselves onto the bridge, we may find that it is not as insubstantial as we fear. Many people have told stories of the strength that can be found in sensing the presence of the infinite, as opposed to merely speculating about it. The weakness, says Okri, is in us, not in the bridge. Our job is to overcome the fear by walking.

When you launch yourself into space or try to tread on the surface of an invisible bridge, what you are really doing is calling the bluff of the vast and seemingly alien universe. You are calling time on all the ruses that keep you comfortable and, so it seems, spiritually empty. What you find is not just rescue from some huge hand or a cunning engineering feat of beams and cables, but something infinitely more valuable. You are taking your place as a rightful inhabitant of creation, a child of God, if you like, and someone whose safety, real safety, has always been guaranteed. And in mid-air, you find that you are not falling at all but soaring.

When life grows flat and empty, have a good look around. When the world betrays you, see if you can't spot a few beams and cables, made of air and feelings. When you despair, you may be a heartbeat away from the bridge. And tell yourself, loud and clear, that it's time to move forward. That's the only game in town. That's why we're here, after all.

Grab the ripcord, call out Geronimo! And learn to fly.

Diving Lessons

Some years ago, I was working with churches in the West Country, and I attended a meeting of ministers and lay pastors in Bridgwater. I hadn't been in those parts long and hadn't yet learned the ropes. During the sharing session I began telling a story I had heard from my psychotherapist. I can't now remember what that was, but it doesn't matter.

After the meeting, a colleague approached me and said in an earnest tone, 'You got away with that here, but for God's sake don't mention it to your congregations.'

'Mention what?' I said.

His answer was embarrassed. 'About seeing your … you know … the, er, therapist.' He had a hard time saying the word. I was astonished.

'Why not?' I asked.

'Because people around here will stop listening to you if they think you are mentally, er, disturbed.'

I tried explaining to him that I didn't consider myself to be mentally disturbed, that I used the experience with my Jungian therapist as a guide to my own inner life and that it was for me a deep spiritual experience.

'That's another thing,' my colleague said. 'Try not to be so *American*.'

Things have changed a lot since then. When I last spoke with this colleague, he was happily burbling about his own therapist. He didn't seem at all American, either. And though it may still be the case that some people attach a sense of shame about getting help from a counsellor or therapist, I find that most people have begun to understand the process a bit better.

I think the problem for most people has sprung from the image of old cigar-chomping Sigmund Freud peering beetle-browed at hysterical patients on a leather divan. Or it may have been the rash of films in the fifties, things like *Lillith* and *The Three Faces of Eve*. Remember those? Oh, and don't forget *Psycho*. The client or patient was always frighteningly insane underneath a calm exterior, and people who needed psychiatrists were dangerous nutters. This sort of image came from the shallow uses to which psychology was being put: people either were psychotic, neurotic or "normal." Everybody wanted to be the third, and went around dreading the second, pretending to be okay even when they weren't.

Things began to change with the work of Carl Gustav Jung. Dissatisfied with the model of the human psyche that Freud had stamped on the new discipline, Jung began to develop a new picture of the mind that went beyond mere cause-and-effect phenomena of the workings of the brain. During a lifetime of personal experimentation, he evolved within the pseudo-scientific discipline of psychology a theory that opened a new door for 20th century thinkers. You might sum it up this way: when he went looking for the causes and cures of neurosis, he bumped into that old and nearly discarded idea – the soul.

Jung saw the human psyche as being much vaster than the limited theory of Freud had allowed for. There was what is called the conscious mind, which, simply put, is everything that we are aware of. That left the unconscious, which, of course, is just everything we are not aware of. His version of the unconscious was not like that of Freud – a kind of swamp of pre-verbal experiences – it was more like a giant sea of a parallel reality, the bottom of which is never found. What is more, Jung found that if you explore deeply enough in the unconscious, you find a place that is *collective.* That is, where each of us touches everything else in the Universe.

He spent years investigating this "collective unconscious", including journeys to China, Africa and Native American communities in the south-western US, where he looked for links in myth and story between completely unconnected cultures. He was on the trail of *archetypes,* the basic building blocks of human consciousness, which figure heavily in the symbols, legends and, yes, the *dreams* of people everywhere.

At the time, Jung was marginalised in a profession that wanted above all to become a respected science like physics or chemistry. On the far opposite end of psychological research, PhDs were inserting electrodes into the brains of cats and dogs and perfecting the horror of electro-shock treatment for mental patients. While they were trying to establish and then enforce a norm for human behaviour, Jung was sailing toward the edge of the world, trying to find the meaning of life.

After his death, other thinkers came forward, psychologists with goals other than the elusive search for the "normal." And they began to combine with an astonishing range of voices from other disciplines, past and present: poets and mystics like Rumi, the founder of Sufi dance, philosophers like William James, physicists like Fitzjoff Capra and even Albert Einstein. They began to re-investigate astrology as a tool for typing personality, worked alongside shamans and tribal medicine men and re-connected with the mystical traditions of the great world religions. Their bookshelves were just as likely to have a copy of the *Bhagavad Gita* as a text of quantum mechanics. The discipline was so new that it didn't have a name, but generally one term began to stick: *transpersonal psychology.* What brought them together was, to put it very simply, the search for God.

After the old white guy with the beard fell off his perch, he left a very big hole in human thinking. Early scientists had ground lenses to peer at him off in space, where Heaven was thought to lie. But they couldn't find him there. Now, when we can gaze on the trillions of galaxies that comprise the universe, he is even less visible to the physical eye. The new wave of thinkers began to listen to older voices which said that God, or the Kingdom of Heaven, or Ultimate Meaning – you choose the synonym that best suits you – that this final source of being lay not "out there" but "in here". And suddenly it seemed that what had begun as a way of controlling the behaviour of crazy people had evolved into a point of resolution of truths from every direction. That was the beginning of what some people call "sacred psychology".

Once you have got the idea that God is to be found within, the whole approach to sacred experience takes on a new form. One definition of the divine is *infinite consciousness.* Sacred psychology turns itself to the gradual unfolding of consciousness from the limited, personal and individual to the infinite, transpersonal and universal. Because none of us are separate from the divine, there must be a route through the consciousness of each of us to the source. What has emerged is that there is indeed a route, but there are no shortcuts.

Sacred psychology would have us re-examine the stories of the ancients, see with new eyes the words of poets and mystics from everywhere in the world and begin a new approach to ritual and ceremony. It would be a mistake to view sacred psychology as a new theory of life. Rather, it is a window through which all the various, sometimes even contrasting, experiences of humanity may be reconciled.

There is a Sufi metaphor that helps me understand all this. It is the image of the pearl diver who wishes to find a precious object. There are various sorts of divers, according to this image. There are those who stand on the beach and gaze longingly at the sea, wishing they had the courage to dive. There are those who actually put their feet into the ocean, but the cold water and strong tides keep them paddling in the shallows. And there are those few, whose longing for the pearl of great price makes them dive deeply, abandoning the safety of dry land.

Sacred psychology is the milieu of the deep diver, those who are willing to go down where things seem dangerous and foreign, into their own inner being. The paddlers are those who have an experience of the sea but are driven back in fear and reluctance. And those who stay on the beach ... well, this is where most of us live our lives, wishing for meaning, knowing where it might lie, but just too timid to take the plunge. This would be all right – there is plenty to do here on the beach, after all – it would be all right except for one thing.

Carl Jung said it, but so did teachers and poets and avatars from every age: there is an unquenchable impulse for consciousness to break through the shell of small self and to know itself finally as the one true Self in all. We have all been on a very long journey, longer than we can imagine. We are more conscious than the seashells at our feet, more conscious than the gulls wheeling overhead, and there is something in us that urges us on, to bring out of the depths of unconsciousness the pearl of final self-awareness. And it just won't let us relax forever on the shore.

Sacred psychology isn't just about theory, though. It is about practice and that toughest task of all; what some call "soul work". For this reason, it doesn't ignore the apparently prosaic demands of ordinary life. In fact, the ordinariness of life is what gives soul work its authority. We can't all just sail off into the wild blue yonder, or, if you prefer, scuba dive straight out of sight. There are children to feed, houses to build, friends to meet, lovers to adore. And it is in just this ordinary arena that the opportunities for real pearl diving emerge.

It is becoming clear to many depth psychologists that symptoms of the mental and physical kind are not just annoyances to be got over. If we are anxious without cause, depressed, gripped by addiction, hobbled by backache, headache, obesity, anorexia, these are not just troubles, but signs from the unconscious part of ourselves. I don't mean to say that all physical symptoms are psychosomatic, far from it. But I do mean that there is something in our condition that is really a kind of soulful road sign that points in the direction of our growth. The way we deal with these things points to the differences between the beachcombers and the deep divers.

At a certain point in life, each of us begins to realise that we are not entirely whole. Why do we avoid certain situations and feel mysteriously fearful when confronted with them? Why does vague illness or fatigue hamper our best-laid plans? Why do we set up circles of collaborators who will tell us how wonderful we are, and wonder why our enemies don't understand us? Why do we set up routines of a magical kind and feel depressed when they are disrupted? Why didn't I write that novel, sail that boat, visit my grandmother in hospital?

I think that there is no one who doesn't have reason to believe that she or he is incomplete or even, in some way, lost. And when this feeling of incompleteness grows strong enough, we turn our eyes toward the sea, where the pearl is submerged. We may "go to see someone" as the euphemism has it. I would prefer to think that the blessing of the symptom has forced us into the deep water, and we have begun to look for the pearl.

This is not an appeal for everyone to rush out and make an appointment with a therapist tomorrow morning. It is a suggestion that each of us begins to look more boldly at the life we have chosen for ourselves and to make an honest appraisal of our needs. And if we find that we are ready to begin to dive for the pearl, we might find someone to go with us, give us diving lessons, hold our hands. If we have begun to see that this journey leads us back to ourselves, not to some unknown destination, we may feel like braving the tall surf. And if we can see that this investigation of the soul is not a medical remedy but a different form of prayer, then we may feel that it is not so different, after all, from what we read these books like this for.

Diving lessons.

Inside Out

I try not to get too upset with the foolish things I see around me. What if new brides are getting tattoos on their necks, where everyone can see, to mark the occasion? What if gender is becoming optional? I'm, like, totes amazeball with all that.

That's because I'm usually an observer. I like to think of myself, as Michel Foucault did, as a kind of archaeologist of the present world. Regular archaeologists get all excited by a shard of pottery or evidence of a cooking fire. I prefer looking through my observer glasses at the strangeness going on around me. It's more comfortable that way. You don't have to approve or disdain; you can just observe and maybe chuckle.

But every once in a while I see something that makes me want to scream. I don't have a dog, or I might, in those moments, kick it a bit. I don't want the neighbours to hear my howl and mistake it for a domestic argument. But there is one thing I can do; preach about it.

Have you seen that TV commercial, the one for BASF? It has the usual will-sapping non-music playing and lots of happy-looking people, balloons, green fields and blue sky. You'd think it was another brainless offering from a retail bank or one of those comparison websites if it didn't begin with these words, "If love is a chemical reaction ..."

Now being a giant chemical conglomerate, it was only a matter of time before some bright spark of an advertising copywriter came up with the misused idea about "chemistry" between two people. But this bland comment has got a deeper edge to it. It assumes that, yes, of course love is about brain chemistry, nothing more. As we get more sophisticated in our scientific techniques, we are able more and more to observe what goes on in the human brain. We discover new enzymes, hormones, yes, chemicals at work in the grey matter. Following tiny electrical impulses with digital equipment straight out of Dr Who, we can measure and record the effect of these chemicals. Then, in logical sequence, we learn how to make some of these chemicals and pump them in where we decide there is a need.

Then, bang! Presto! We can make someone happy, sleepy, dopey – any one of the seven dwarves that you like. Sneezy, even. If you're depressed, there's a chemical that will help. Yes, it really will help. If you're lethargic, another one will make you active. If you're just not in a party mood, we can provide a sensation of ecstasy. It's all true – go ask Alice, when she's ten feet tall.

Most of that is in fact a welcome advance. We need to use whatever we can to make things better. That's what we humans have always done, more or less. But the underside of the advance is a new and frightening idea. That idea is that the highest and most sublime experiences do not spring from somewhere that is in itself high and exalted, but from a mix of chemicals. In other words, everything is artificial, and everything can be subject to manipulation.

Now I'm going to tell you a few things that will never appear on my CV. In my youth, in the nineteen-sixties, I took a lot of drugs. Not fun drugs, not heroin or cocaine, and certainly not the little pills you can buy tonight in any dance club in London. When I was just twenty, I took a very large dose of peyote, the hallucinogen derived from a variety of cactus, the same one that inspired Don Juan, the Mexican guru. I experienced something that is quite literally beyond description, so that I probably shouldn't even try. I didn't know what I was getting myself into. I think I imagined that I would see red gorillas in pink fluffy jungles or something like that. But what happened to me was much more profound. I had taken the peyote alone, something advised against by nearly everyone.

For a few hours, I was nauseated. I got the idea that I was going to die. I wrote a note that begged forgiveness of everyone I had ever offended, left my few possessions to a couple of friends and signed off. But before I could finish, I realised that I was, in a sense that defies explanation, already dead. I was suspended in air near the roof of an enormous cathedral, held up by beams of light that streamed from stained glass windows of unbelievable colour and beauty. I saw myself as part of what I think of as pure consciousness and soon realised that the same consciousness was not only IN everyone else, but that we were all composed of the same consciousness. My feeling? Well, to say "joy" wouldn't begin to describe it, but that's as far as the English language can take me. Joy and ... OK, love.

It took about six hours before I began to see that I was actually squatting on the floor of my dormitory room. I had missed lectures, meals and telephone messages. A friend came round, and I spent a futile hour trying to explain to him what had happened to me. The following morning I felt fine and went back to class, saw my pals and did all the normal things. But I was changed.

What followed was a marathon effort of reading. People like William James and his *Varieties of Religious Experience.* Writers like Allan Watts. Zen masters like D T Suzuki. Even the western saints like Theresa and John of the Cross. I was obsessed with the idea that I had had an experience that was not unknown in the literature, an experience usually referred to as "mystical". I met other people who had shared the experience. I began taking LSD. I went to see Timothy Leary and Richard Alpert (now called Baba Ram Dass) in New York. Finally, I came upon a statement by Meher Baba: "If God can be found through taking a pill, God is not worthy of being God."

In later years, I learned that he had authenticated the experiences as resembling those of true mysticism, but that they were useless as a tool for self-knowledge. The reason was that they happened in an inside-out way. The brain chemistry did in fact change in the way it might if you were able to examine a genuine mystic at the height of an experience, but this was so because the mystic's chemical changes followed awareness; they did not cause the awareness. People who find themselves in a state that resembles mystical ecstasy without, as it were, having earned their way there were just tourists, in a sense. The insights gained could not possibly be used to determine behaviour.

As soon as I heard this, I knew that Meher Baba knew what he was talking about and stopped taking psychedelic drugs. I know that he was right. That's why I hate that BASF advert, and if there were any realistic way of boycotting their products, I would do it. Here's why.

We're living in a time in which science has gained the upper hand. Books like *The Selfish Gene* attempt to explain such things as love as the result of genetic codes that prompt our brains to care about our offspring and mates, because that is a survival strategy for the species. Richard Dawkins sounds apologetic and even wistful as he unintentionally disposes of millennia of poetry, religious experience and self-sacrifice. The mantra is as always: if something cannot be scientifically verified, weighed and measured, then it cannot be said to exist. In philosophy, this is called materialism. Not the word we use to describe wanting a new car, but a world view. If a feeling of love or ecstasy can be mimicked by giving an injection or stimulus with an electrode, then that – by scientific logic – proves that that is ALL it is. Just a tweaking of the forebrain that changes everything.

These are the same guys who regularly burgle our simple experiences of something transcendent. Sunset is merely dust motes in the atmosphere refracting slanted light. A baby's gurgle of recognition for their mother is merely a biological prompting from a gene. Stirring music, like hymns, are merely the sonic activation of serotonin molecules in the cerebrum or somewhere. But even as they give us this bad news, they attempt to make it all better by standing on a mountaintop in a TV science programme, waving their arms towards the night sky and saying, 'Isn't that enough?'

Well, no. It's not.

Let's go back to that interesting little clue Meher Baba was giving us. The difference between outside and inside. By outside, I mean everything you can weigh or measure and explain purely by scientific means. By inside, I mean a reality hinted at by legions of sages and saints through history, a separate reality that coincides with the one we can see and feel but that is not dependent upon it I mean that there is a difference between the mind and the brain. The brain is a mass of tissue, the mind is the source of consciousness. If you do something to the brain, through injury, illness or by using drugs, it affects the mass of tissue, but not what I'm calling the mind. In this way of looking at things, the brain, the eyes and ears and indeed the whole body are means by which the mind, the awareness that makes a person, experiences the world.

So why aren't we aware of this other reality, you might ask. I would say that you are aware of it, that what you think of as your life is dependent upon it. Things like love. Love is the awareness, however feeble, of oneness. It is the diminution of the isolated self, the sense that you are in some way living in two centres, where the boundaries of *me* intermingle with those of *thee.*

Being determined to find simple explanations for things like love, scientists, not all, but some, are mining the brain for something they call "the God spot". This would be the final cap on the victory of mere materialism – a little gland somewhere that has made people in all ages and all places exhibit a concept of God. So far, the brain miners have had no luck. But even if they do find it tucked into the hypothalamus or somewhere, it won't change anything. The gulf between inside and outside will still rule OK.

If you were God, how would you design your universe? Would you make your existence provable in a science lab? Would you lay down tablets of stone that had only to be read and obeyed to solve the problem of existence? Or, instead, would you make human beings so that they had to leave behind their toys of analysis and do a search the hard way, through the heart? Would you leave the instruction manual on the outside, or tuck it away inside, where only the real pilgrims would look for it?

"If love is a chemical reaction ..." caws the BASF commercial. If love is a chemical reaction, that is, *merely* a chemical reaction, then God is not only non-existent, He's not worthy of being God.

... And a Time to Change

I could add something to that famous list from Ecclesiastes. You know the one I mean: "... a time to love and a time to hate; a time to build and a time to tear down." Etcetera. I wish he'd also said that there is also a time to change and a time to stay the same.

I can sympathise with people like me, who apparently have no reason to want things to change very much. Because I'm very, very lucky.

I'm white. Actually, a kind of mottled pink, but you get the idea. Even though things are changing, that's still the fast ticket to power and success in the unjust world we inhabit. I'm male. Yes, fellas, like it or not, that still gives us an edge. We may try to deny it, may get weary of feminists going on about it, but it's true. I'm also a member of that big majority that refers to itself as more or less straight; heterosexual, even though I have good reason to doubt that anything is as black and white as that. But if you don't think that's an advantage, just ask some of our friends in the gay Ugandan refugee community. And I grew up in the richest and most powerful country in the world. That determined my attitudes, some of which are so deeply engrained in me that I occasionally shock myself.

Given all that, I'm the last person in the world who should be able to stand up and preach about justice. So I should just shut up and sit down. I would, I really would, if I knew I could stick it. But I'm feeling restless. It's like sitting in a room with a painting on the wall that's hanging crooked. Wonky, I believe you call it in this rich British way. You can try to ignore it, but, finally, you'll get out of your chair and try to fix it.

Now, the things I see that need changing can't be fixed by me as easily as straightening a wonky picture. It's likely that they can't be fixed at all, at least not in this lifetime. I can't even be sure that, as Lao Tse once warned, I won't make things even worse.

But this much, at least, needs to be said: *Something is wrong.*

Something is wrong when urban teenagers shoot and stab each other over childish ideas of respect and territory. Something is wrong when policemen shoot or strangle people they want to arrest for minor or non-existent crimes. Something is wrong when infants in African countries die of dehydration under the gaze of millions of TV viewers. Something is wrong when kids in poor countries are starving and kids in rich countries are contracting fatal diseases from obesity. Something is wrong when the saddest imaginable television programme about the Syrian disaster is interrupted eight times an hour to show the stock prices on world markets to find out early about the next financial stampede. Something is wrong when a banker is paid 20 million pounds while pensioners are denied home care, and council tenants in wheelchairs have to pay a bedroom tax invented by a man who lives in a seven-bedroom mansion.

Something is wrong when we know that the cradle of the world's atmosphere is growing dangerous, that we are already beginning to cook ourselves to death and still work overtime to buy a 4-litre SUV, and scheme yet new ways to drag carbon fuels from the rocks beneath our green and pleasant land. Something is wrong when fever to grow rich through buy-to-rent schemes has made neighbourhoods unaffordable to those who grew up in them. Something is wrong when we co-conspire with leaders who sing us the old lullaby about ever-growing economies, and ever-increasing wealth, while the stony earth is fertilised by the bodies of victims of the so-called free market in countries we have scarcely heard of.

Something is wrong when we encourage resentment from the poorest among us, about even poorer people coming to live and work in Barking or Sheffield or Cardiff, and do it for narrow political aims. Something is wrong when people who are born to love those of their own gender find an uncertain welcome when they flee from real danger in their homelands, to find only grudging accommodation here. Something is wrong when, in order to further the dominance of the financial sector, we invite international criminals to bring us their money and implicitly endorse dictators around the world.

Something is wrong when pensioners in their thousands have to choose between heating and eating. No need to go into a complicated song and dance about the economy or the structure of the oil and gas industry. Let's just tell it like it is – that's *wrong*.

You can add to the list. Go ahead, if you want to. Or just nod. *Something is wrong.*

Okay. That's the easy part. We all know that already. It may be that everyone really knows it on some level. However well we practise the sham of denial, things creep in. And, like dogs who bark just before an earthquake, maybe our cries born of stress and depression are the same thing, after all. Unease seems to afflict almost everyone. The disappearance of old values and unshakable certainties have left us vulnerable to quick fixes and shallow insights.

Most of us, including me, deal with all this by ignoring it. We have our ways: distraction with amusements, self-serving denial and blame-casting in any other direction.

Some of us deal with unease by becoming fundamentalists. America is full of that right now. The drone of background anxiety is driving people to places where charismatic voices assure them that they are favoured by God and that the excesses of their lives are their just rewards. Even the threat of global war is sanitised and made attractive in this drive-in mass religious culture. Dig a few half-baked words from a scripture that was assembled by people with their own political agendas and convince everyone that the Plain of Armageddon is something to be looked forward to. Wait for rapture, but don't spare yourself the fried chicken while you do.

Then there are others who find their way to mosques where the ancient holy words of Islam are made into the equivalent of Chairman Mao's Little Red Book, and the slaughter of innocents is turned into a holy act. In the lives of the young suicide bombers we see the contentment of people who don't have to wonder any more, for whom the burden of choice and reason has become as remote a problem as teenage acne. Faces shining with glory, they proclaim themselves holy warriors, and the commuters of London and the pedestrians of Mumbai the enemy.

But their real spiritual kinsmen are not in Mecca. They are in Kansas and Idaho, just as convinced that shooting a doctor at an abortion clinic is serving Christ. Their eyes shine in the same way; their arguments are the same. Their anointing has been the same, too. Like the psychotic who has what is called a "paranoid insight", they have welded feelings of personal inadequacy and disappointment to an irrational fantasy that is wholly logic-tight. Meaning, that sweet but all-too-elusive element, has been cast in stone. *Halleluia! Allah u Akbar!* The slogans are one and the same.

It seems that maybe it is God Himself who is to blame. After all, every bit of this mayhem seems to be done in His name. And if the fanatics are full of passionate intensity, as W B Yeats once said, do we really lack all conviction?

We have made a new God out of our own wishfulness. That God somehow is made to co-exist with the one that we have been taught to worship, the one of Jesus and Mohammed and Krishna and the great Sufi masters. If Jesus says, "When a man asks for your coat, give him your shirt as well," the new God says, "Don't raise taxes or investment will cease." If he says, "Behold the lilies of the field", that becomes "reducing the deficit to protect a triple A rating in the bond market". The old God is kept locked up in churches and mosques; the new one roams the Square Mile and Wall Street. God's in his Heaven; the market rules OK.

If I'm criticising the competitive marketplace as a yardstick of morality, maybe we can find some clues in the ancient wisdom of our culture, in places like the Old Testament. I'm speaking now of the tradition of judges in ancient Israel, who made justice a living, not an abstract phenomenon.

In the West, we have a concept of justice inherited from the Greeks and Romans. On top of some of our most august chambers of law, you will find a blindfolded statue, holding a sword in one hand and a set of scales in the other. Justice needs, we think, to be blind, to use abstract fairness, scientifically derived by devices which never lie, like the scales. It is absolute, "fair". But in ancient Hebrew civilisation, judges were not blindfolded but gifted with sharp vision. The idea was not just to see who was right and who was wrong in a matter, but to look deeply into the human situation, to determine what must be done to make matters right: to heal rather than punish, integrate rather than discriminate.

If the ancient Jews can't convince us, let's go to those words of Western scripture called *The Merchant of Venice* and consult the prophet Shakespeare about the rightness or wrongness of debt and repayment. This is the famous "pound of flesh" scene, where the lender Shylock is told: "The quality of mercy is not strained. It droppeth as the gentle rain from heaven upon the place beneath: it is twice blessed; it blesseth him that gives and him that takes ..." And, in these telling words, the Bard says, "... In the course of justice, none of us should see salvation ..."

But we must make sure we balance the budget. It would be nice to think we could just pour money on all the world's poor, ensure everyone in our cities has a reason to get up in the morning, and end the oppression of wealth gone mad. But that's foolish, isn't it? Foolish like Jesus, say, and we know what happened to him. Financial probity is the ultimate gauge of morality, isn't it? Isn't economic justice just what is left over after everyone has had their profits? Isn't it? Maybe we should ask ourselves if penny wisdom really isn't pound foolishness. Are we really asking how much it will cost to do justice? Is there any real choice?

So here's what I think we must do: take the cold words of the politicians and money men with a pinch of salt, not a pound of flesh. Begin to wonder if there aren't things we might be able to live without or pay more for in order to make fair choices. Where there is misery, reach deep, stump up. Look with unclouded vision at the unfairness of our institutions. Complain about things that are just plain *wrong.*

The cold logic of the marketplace can give only short-term benefits; it is fuelled by the basest of human emotions, whatever gloss the idealists of money-making want to put on it. But the logic of mercy, of caring, of the soul is by its very nature of long-term value. If you doubt that, think for a moment of the way you feel when you have been shrewd and cunning in a business deal, and compare that with the feeling of warmth that accompanies a selfless act of some kind, when the payoff was not in your bank account, but on the face of the beneficiary. In your last moments, which one would you prefer?

One more question, the first that was ever asked by a person in the Old Testament: "Am I my brother's keeper?"

Is it just me, or is that a no-brainer?

Why?

If you want to pique the interest of someone, really get their ears up, there is one really, sure-fire way to do it: you can offer them some secret that claims it will change their lives.

It can be almost anything. A code-breaking approach to ancient texts, for example, that proves that Moses was in touch with an alien super-race that has wonderful plans for humanity. A way to lose two stone of unpleasant-looking fat from your body that doesn't require surgery. It can be a new cure-all medicine, like the snake oil sold to nearly everybody gullible enough to believe it in the nineteenth century United States. If you think snake oil is dead these days, have a look at some of the alternative medicines promoted on the Internet.

Sometimes people have a blinding flash of insight about life, the universe and all that. This is sometimes referred to as getting saved. When I was twelve, I went to a presentation one night at the local high school by a pseudo-scientific fundamentalist preacher doing something called "Sermons from Science". I went with my pal Mike Fields and his parents. I can't remember much about it, except that sharks never go to sleep and that there were slides of mastodons unearthed from the ice with un-chewed grass in their mouths, proving that the Flood came upon them suddenly, while Noah was riding the waves in his ark. Heady stuff.

I remember being flooded with light. I was saved! So were lots of others. At the end of the show, we were taken into a room and signed up, given pledging envelopes and prayed over. Meanwhile, the Fields family sat fuming and un-saved, waiting in the car. I think I stayed saved until the following Thursday, and I haven't been saved since. But my parents got mail pleas for donations for several years afterwards.

I'd like to think that I have outgrown that gullibility, that we all have, but it's sadly not the case. It's as if the hungry human mind has got an expectation of life-changing revelation hard-wired into it. We're always ready to invent the wheel or see the future in a pattern of animal entrails.

It's just part of us. In fact, if it were not so, I don't think there would be a single person in any church this morning.

So I might as well just confess it up front: ministers don't have any magical secrets or special formulas to offer. If that's a disappointment, I'm sorry. You may well ask, if you don't have answers for us, why are you writing this book? What's the use of listening to you if you can't provide remedies for life's problems? That's a tough question, and believe me, one I have asked myself often. If I were asked it in some post-death tribunal way up yonder, I suppose I would have to answer like this: we're all in the same boat. We don't believe in snake oil or nine-day programs to become giants; that's not why we're here.

We're here, God bless us, because we feel that answers come from within the boat, even though it often seems to be foundering in the heaving tide of meaninglessness and relativity. We aren't going to find stone tablets that decode reality or burning bushes that tell us secrets. Whatever we find out about life, the universe and all that, we will find within the baffling experience that we all share. We feel that the answer to life, if any, can only be found within it. We feel, as so many of the great voices from spiritual tradition have told us, that life may be a kind of school – all about learning.

What do I mean by *learning?* This is not about something that is merely descriptive. It aims deeper, and I think it points to the *why* of things. This is important to us, because, if you think about it, the questions about *what* or *how* are fleeting. You may lose some sleep over bills you can't pay, or wrestle with your own instincts about weight loss or career plans, but the questions that shake you awake at six in the morning and grab you with the icy touch of death are the ones about *why* – the *why* of everything.

In the last few years we have been treated to a welter of popular theories from physicists, mathematicians, even biologists, like Richard Dawkins, for example. In their furious need to explain everything, or perhaps to explain it *away,* they have done what can only be seen as metaphysical claim-jumping. Hence we have autopsies and electrode experiments looking for what has been called the "God node" in the human brain – the reason why the concept of God uniquely occurs to human beings. In a recent television programme, a mathematician wound up suicidally depressed when he was told by a man who put him into a brain scanner, that all his decisions, the very root of what is called free will, were predetermined by the shape of his brain.

I'm not anti-scientific in any real sense. I like most of the scientists I have known. I find them earnest and charmingly enthusiastic. I'm certainly not opposed to the technology that, for example, saved the sight of my right eye a few years ago and has made marvellous new hip joints for a lot of my friends. What wearies me is the misuse of that three-letter word they employ so readily when they say, "This is *why* such and such a phenomenon takes place." I feel that they don't mean "why" at all, but a complicated version of "how".

The ancient Greek philosopher Aristotle described four kinds of "why". I forget the first ones, but the last two are very interesting, and should perhaps be integrated into the curriculum of any budding scientist. They are "efficient cause" and "final cause." Efficient cause is linked to the idea of agency: what it is that happens to make something else happen. For example, the car's brakes failed, causing an accident. But "final cause" is a bit more complex, and way outside the scope of scientific research, at least as we know it so far. Final cause would answer the question "why was it necessary for the car to crash?" In other words, the meaning and significance of the event, not just a description of it.

When the scientific method becomes the single lodestone of human knowledge, as it seems to have done lately, we are stuck one level too far back. We get caught up in an endless loop of "how", when what our hearts long for is an answer to the bigger question: "why". I remember one Christmas Eve of my childhood asking my father why a furniture truck had just struck and killed my dog. He began to answer by saying that maybe Tim had grown too deaf to hear the truck as it approached. But I wanted more, and asked him again, 'Why?' Catching my meaning, which was that most plaintive human query of all, he said, 'Son, I don't know.'

When I have been called upon to deal with people who have suddenly become bereaved, I go through all the things I was taught in counselling and ministry training. I sit with them in their grief, as much as I am able, and try to offer the pale comfort of another person's presence. But it's never very long until that same question emerges, the one question that lies at the very heart of the human condition: *why?*

There are psychotherapists who believe, and I agree, that most psychological problems come back to the *why* of things. The name of this is logotherapy, but that doesn't really matter. It holds that people who present themselves with problems of relationship, depression, addictions and a host of other symptoms have one thing in common: what underlies them is a lack of meaning in their lives. And this is like some major flu pandemic of the modern world. You don't have to be an alcoholic or a shoplifter to have it, we all do.

And yes, there are many who offer quick fixes to this universal problem, ways of distracting oneself with hobbies, love affairs, patriotism, new cars. We are familiar with all this; we all do it. It may be efficient for a while, may offer some soothing music to drown out the drone of the constant question we might hear if we listened: Why? What does it all mean? What's the point?

How hard we work to avoid hearing this question! How much we fear its being asked, and how we resist when it snatches us out of bed or descends upon us in a doctor's surgery or seems to float in the air of autumn like the leaves from the unprotesting trees. But sometimes, when we simply cannot avoid it, the question grips us. This moment is not just an affliction but a gift. Just as crises always bear a secret benefit of opportunity, I think that the question of meaning, or the sense of its absence, carries with it something of our birth-right, a treasure waiting to be discovered.

Learning depends upon the question "why." Education, as we have come to know it, may respond to questions of *how* or *what* as we substitute training for real learning. As Paolo Freire reportedly said, "You train a donkey, but you educate a person." The *hows* and *whats* were not so important to Socrates or Lao Tse; the *whys* were. If you teach somebody to be a barber or a brain surgeon, you have still not even scratched the surface of learning about the real questions.

No, for that, you need a better teacher. Socrates is long dead; we cannot replace him with a panel of PhDs. For real learning, nothing beats life itself. Most of the great spiritual teachers have said this. Life is just a big old school, one in which every sentient being has a guaranteed place, just by being born. For curriculum we have that staggering myriad of experiences;

for resources, we have the gift of consciousness. As to the teacher, well, you may take your pick of ideas. For me, I am content to say that God does that. That which in our essence we really are, from which we have sprung and to which we return without ever having been separate from it – that's a long way of saying the same thing. There are bright pupils and dim ones, swots and truants, those who take their exams on time and those who skive off, but no one is left out. Everybody graduates. Not only that: everybody gets an A, sooner or later. So what's the hurry?

Sharks continue to swim in the sea, wide awake. The scientific establishment may continue going on about the Higgs boson, and we may go out and get saved this afternoon or buy a new car. But the bell hasn't rung yet; we are all still learning the three R's of existence, and we will do it until we get it right.

So the next time something wakes you, prods or scares you, makes your palms sweat or calls upon more than you have ever imagined yourself capable of, don't worry. It's only life, doing what it was intended to do: help us learn. Don't run from it: it's too fast. Don't ignore it: it's too insistent. And don't fear it: it's what we're all about.

The Chase

How's it going?

That's the way Americans greet each other. Over here in Britain, we tend to say, "You all right?" Nearly the same thing but maybe pointing to a subtle difference.

The Declaration of Independence, written by Jefferson and other rebels in the American colonies, makes claims to what life is all about: life, liberty and the pursuit of happiness. Having acknowledged that happiness is something you have to pursue, Americans tend to enquire about each other that way: "How's the pursuit going?"

Believe it or not, there is such a thing as the Global Happiness Index, which rates countries according to their own experience of happiness and its opposite. The happiest country in the world this year is ... right; Finland. The least happy alternates between a handful of African and Middle Eastern countries who are in perpetual war. It's a dodgy way to try and unravel everyone's experience of life, but it does seem to make at least some sense. We aren't the happiest lot in the world, but we're not too bad. Same with the US. But I believe that, at least in America, you rate yourself on how the pursuit of happiness is going, and that most often means personal wealth.

Think about it. You're born, hairless and with no sharp claws or teeth. You get a brain, which starts to cause you problems from the very start. You are full of desires that can never be fulfilled. What's more, you know from early on about your own inevitable death. You live half in the past through memories, and half in the future, through anticipation. How are you supposed to find happiness with that sort of kit?

However you answer that question, the interesting thing is that it is only recently in human history that that sentence would have had very much meaning. Happiness in life throughout much of the past would have been the payoff for appeasing wrathful and pernickety gods. The question of happiness would have meant something like, "Have you got enough to eat tonight?" It was a mystery whether or not you'd live to be an old man or woman of thirty, or if God would strike you down with something like a tooth abscess or a sabre-toothed tiger.

After that, for most of history, happiness became a secondary concern for people. When survival is an issue, happiness is a remote idea, except for things like full bellies and relative safety from attack. As the social psychologist, Abram Maslow, pointed out with his famous pyramid, it's not likely you'll be thinking about self-fulfilment if you're not getting enough to eat.

What the early Enlightenment claimants to happiness, like the authors of the Declaration of Independence, were probably referring to was more of the same: material happiness. A warm safe bed and enough to eat were already beyond the expectations of all the centuries past; more refined notions of spiritual satisfaction were the obsessions of poets and the idle rich. But as material well-being grew through the nineteenth century, ideas of happiness of a more absolute sort appeared. Poets such as Blake and Wordsworth in England sounded a warning that mere materialism wasn't going to result in the attainment of happiness, after all. Fulfilment did lie in this world, but not through the accretion of wealth. It had more to do with a process of self-cultivation, an idea originally foreseen by the precocious Greeks.

Thus began a time of seeking for fulfilment that today has become a major obsession. The post-modernist philosopher Michel Foucault termed the self-help and human potential movement "technologies of the self". That is, a series of processes enacted by the person upon the person with the aim of some kind of transformation. In other words, a version of the pursuit of happiness. The examples are legion: *How to Win Friends and Influence People,* Reiki, macrobiotic diet, primal scream therapy, neuro-linguistic programming, astrology, orgone boxes, re-birthing, Rolfing, the Enneagram, ginseng, automatic writing, crystal healing, LSD. Have I forgotten a few? Numerology, spiritual autobiography, kundalini yoga, sweat lodges, Iron John, circle dancing, reflexology, Bach flower remedies, tree hugging, sensory deprivation, ley line walking, aromatherapy. I'm getting tired. There are probably a thousand of these that I haven't mentioned; you can find out the next time there's a Body, Mind and Spirit Fair at Earl's Court.

I'm not knocking any of these activities; I may do a few of them myself. The point is that we have become obsessive about the pursuit of elusive happiness. We feel that there must be some ancient trick or some arduous procedure that will open the gates for us and make us happy. More: we may have begun to feel a little desperate; the right to happiness is beginning to look like the *duty* to be happy. It is uncool to display emptiness and to be unhappy.

So, it is interesting that whereas once people conceived of attaining happiness simply as a matter of getting more and more stuff, there is a recent trend that focuses on transformation. Not that materialism has suffered much. Getting and spending is still enjoying mass popularity, despite the recession. But there are a growing number of us that feel happiness needs to be sought through changing ourselves in some way. Maybe because our parents didn't do something well in our infancy. Maybe because capitalism degrades, or because the Druids are gone. Maybe it's because we have a block in our chi or aren't *feng shui* enough. Whatever the reason, there is something that needs changing, healing, transforming.

And we tell ourselves little tales: "We'll be happy when we pay off the mortgage. Graduate and get a degree. Get published. Have that face lift. Because we think: how can I be happy when I'm old? Got arthritis? Am too fat? But if you think about the times when you were, to steal a phrase, surprised by joy, you had all those problems then, too. And the happiness appeared anyway. So – could it be that happiness has nothing to do with relief from our constant problems and complaints?

Happiness seems to elude us. The hurrier we chase it, the behinder we get. Could it be that this is because, not only do we not know what we want, but we wouldn't recognise it if it sat in our laps? How many times have we said, that was probably the happiest time of my life? Meaning, perhaps, that we didn't know it at the time. Maybe we don't know what happiness is like. Maybe we should take some advice from a few old-fashioned experts.

Plato and his teacher Socrates seemed to have a fairly decent idea about earthly happiness. In one discourse, he talks about the difference between pleasure and happiness. This known as the "argument of the leaky jug." A Hedonist tried to claim that happiness is found in the accumulation of pleasure and the avoidance of pain. He said that life is like a jug with a hole in it. The water you pour in is pleasure; the water that leaks out is pain. The trick is to pour in more pleasure than you experience pain. That's the way to be happy.

Plato took him gently through a series of Socratic questions that differentiate pleasure from happiness. His point is that happiness has more to do with a relationship to what he called the Real than to the distraction of the senses. In other words, happiness is not created but *found.* When something is found, it cannot be non-existent; it must have been there all along, lying just out of sight.

The rabbi Jesus took it even further. His sermons were full of paradox: gaining one's life is losing it; living is found through dying, and other brain teasers. He made a point of saying that seeking wealth – trying to stave off suffering through accumulation – came at the cost of one's soul. This was more than the hair-shirt masochism of certain religious orders, because all the evidence points to a rather merry Jesus who enjoyed good wine and interesting companions. And happiness did not just lie in the sweet by-and-by of some of his more life-hating subsequent followers: the Kingdom of Heaven was "at hand", right here and now, if only we could be bothered to see it.

Meher Baba used to frustrate the seekers that gathered around him. For one thing, he didn't speak for the more than forty years that preceded his death. He indicated that there had been a great plenty of words said throughout history, to very little real effect. Also, he gave few orders and asked for little technique in the spiritual search. He did offer general advice to all seekers of truth, however. He said, "Don't worry. Be happy." He said that long before the Reggae song, by the way. Once, when someone seemed to take the phrase lightly, Baba gestured sternly that the order was serious. To worry was to underestimate God, and to be happy was the most sincere way to pray.

There's something there that has always intrigued me. The statement says that the opposite of happiness is worry. Even the World Happiness Index used worry as the opposite of happiness on its graphs. Worry is that famous thing that does no good, changes nothing. So here's the formula for success: happiness equals freedom from worry.

Included in this idea is a simple truth. Worry cannot be defeated by arranging things so carefully that nothing bad can happen. It can only be banished by the worrier who, noticing the futility of worrying, simply stops doing it.

Being asked to be happy, not to worry, without any good reason is a tough one, isn't it? On the face of it, it seems, if not impossible, a little mindless. It's like being asked to leapfrog over yourself, and wind up at your destination before you make your journey.

Since happiness is not made, but found, the question becomes, "Where do we find it?" And the answer, given thousands of times, over and over, by the great voices of every generation, seem to say, "It's right here. Just open your eyes and see." Happiness is not just your birth-right, it is who you really are. Don't worry. Be happy. Don't try to make yourself safe from calamity. Don't brainwash yourself with slogans and emotionalism disguised as worship. Just do it.

Or as Meher Baba also said, "Cheerfulness is a gift to your companions." I take that to mean that happiness is somewhat contagious. It spreads the same way as gloom. And I've come to believe something else: happiness, joy – use your own word – is the appearance of the holy.

So, could it be that the idea of pursuing happiness is a false trail? You can mentally picture a billionaire or a movie star or best-selling author miserably chasing the next deal, the next honour, the next reward that will, finally, satisfy. You can look inward and see that, too.

Maybe we should stop pursuing happiness. Maybe we should just stop and let it catch us.

First the Bad News

Did you ever have one of those days when something you thought you knew turned out not to be true? I had one of those this week. I was disappointed when I learned that one of my favourite little trick expressions is based on a false interpretation of Chinese.

The little trick expression is the claim that the Chinese symbol for our word "crisis" is composed of two smaller words: "danger" and "opportunity". This has been the basis for all sorts of optimistic books, New Age courses and business management seminars. I have used it in a sermon, long ago. I just hope it's not somewhere on the Internet.

The Chinese version of crisis is actually composed of the symbol for danger and one which means something like "things change". I was disappointed to discover this because I do feel that the muddle we human beings have got ourselves in recently might just represent an opportunity. It certainly will presage a change.

Science fiction writers have long speculated that the only way to unify the warring and competing factions of the human race would be a common enemy. A Martian invasion would do the trick. Maybe a rogue asteroid would do. We would all have to hang together in the face of a looming common danger, or all hang separately. The bitter feuds and hatred would be set aside. Sunni and Shia Muslims would fall into each other's arms. Catholics and Protestants in Northern Ireland would embrace. Vladimir Putin and Barack Obama would have each other over to dinner. And the inevitability of one world government would fall into place at last.

The latest news flash is that no aliens have been spotted. We're not expecting any asteroids for a few hundred years, according to astronomers. What we seem to be facing instead is an environmental catastrophe in the form of climate change. The problem is that the thing is taking so long to happen, or so we think. So long that we can't even be sure it's happening at all.

That may be because climate change, and what, if anything, to do about it, has met with a lot of resistance from ordinary people. Now there are what are called "climate change deniers", people who doubt that any such thing exists. Or, if it does exist, is the result of natural processes, sunspots or cyclical change.

Here's a conversation I had recently with a cab driver. I should have been alerted when I saw him toss an empty drink container onto the street.

'Warm, isn't it?' I say.

'About normal for this time of year,' he responds. I imagine that I detect a note of defensiveness in his voice.

'Not global warming, then,' I say.

'No such thing.'

'You're not bothered by all the talk about climate change?'

'That's a load of old cobblers. When I was a kid, we had much hotter weather than this.'

'You think they're making it all up, then? Why would they do that?'

He glances at me in the mirror. 'Any way they can pick on the car driver, they'll do. Raise the petrol price, put speed bumps everywhere so that you ruin your suspension, anything they can think of.'

'Because?'

'It's money, innit? Jobs for the boys.'

That's a tempting position. Wouldn't it be great if the whole thing was just some scientists trying to get famous or rich? That's denial writ very large, and denial is always more comfortable than eyeballing the truth; that's why we do it. It's a cushion against what would otherwise be unbearable. I think of these people as "flat-earthers".

Then there are the guilt-mongers. These are modern day cousins of Luddites and maybe some 17th century puritans, who see the looming disasters as something like a divine punishment for human greed. The fact that many of them are atheists doesn't mean that they're not subject to the sin and punishment syllogism that Bible thumpers have always employed. We've been too greedy, with our machines and our neon lights. Pretty soon they'll come around your house and peek in your bins to make sure you're cooperating.

Then there are the rest of us. Thinking that the scientists are probably right but feeling helpless to do much about it other than a spot of recycling and changing light bulbs. Too politically correct to be caught out scoffing at the predictions, but too lost in our own lives to get any traction on the solution.

If you're like me, you don't think a lot about carbon emissions and global warming. If you look up at the sky on one of our rare cloudless days, it looks just fine. But we can't see carbon atoms; we can't see the microbes that wipe out whole populations, either, so we just have to take the scientists' word for it. And that would be fine, except nobody, absolutely nobody, knows what to do about it.

So we turn down our thermostats a few dutiful notches, replace old light bulbs with those things you can't really see anything by for at least five minutes, and wait. Polar bears appear on our TV screens like sweet fairy tale beings instead of the most feared land predator on earth, and we watch the breaking ice floes and feel terrible. Maps of the vanishing Amazon rainforest haunt us, and the doomster film makers have used computer generated images to stop our hearts with fear.

Ask a politician or an economist and they will give you a story about industry and jobs. Somebody gets paid to make the complex little plastic books that fresh herbs are sold in, and somebody else gets paid to bring them to the supermarket from Turkey or Zimbabwe. Someone else gets paid to operate the printing machines on the cartons of frozen dinners, and then the dustmen get paid to carry it away. Try to remove any part of it and there will be unemployment in Scarborough or Schenectady or strikes in shipping ports. The whole mad dance requires us to participate or die.

This is our condition now, after a century or two of dazzling scientific advance. Soon now, they'll be able to clone us at birth and leave spare body parts floating in a tank until we need them. We'll be able to put our eyeballs against a screen and have our goods charged to some central computer bank. The muggers can kill you for your smart phone, but not for your cash, because there won't be any; a small microchip inserted into the flesh of the elbow will do instead. If we are still able to die, we can have our ashes dispersed in space, as if there wasn't already enough stuff floating around up there. We'll have all this, that is, unless we've overlooked something vital.

Maybe we can blame all this on Darwin. After all, it was he who identified our animal origins and linked us with them. It was others who made philosophical hay out of it, claiming as did Mrs Thatcher that the survival of the fittest was the moral law of humanity. We hear that competitive self-interest is the great mover of history; obeying our genetic impulses to get more things for ourselves is the route to progress. The rallying cry of the masses is "more, more!" and only losers might say, "Enough, already."

Perhaps we can't help it. After all, most of human history has been a story of not having enough, so that there was no occasion to learn restraint. When I lived in Botswana some years ago, along with the staggering scenery, it was impossible not to notice the litter along the roads. Everywhere you looked there were aluminium cans tossed aside by those who could afford cold drinks. It was an eyesore, but I realised that there had never until then been anything in African life that didn't decompose naturally where it was dropped; eggshells, nut shells, bits of leather and wood all rot.

Like the village Africans, we have always relied on the forces of nature to sort things out. Until fairly recently, we couldn't do enough damage to the planet if we tried to bring on a crisis. We needed no internal regulator because we were too weak to do much harm. We had to build our towns charmingly perched on hillsides, with picturesque winding streets and squares. Now we can lop off the top of a mountain and dump it in a valley and make a housing estate with phoney half-timbered buildings, and we do. They are not as nice to look at, and so the richest among us paradoxically seek the charm of earlier, less technologically efficient times. Thatched houses in Surrey with priest holes, say. We don't like the look of our new neighbourhoods any more than we like the taste of Big Macs, but that doesn't stop us.

I said earlier that I still thought that danger might represent opportunity, even if the Chinese symbol doesn't say so. Our own word comes from the Greek, meaning "turning point in a disease". Things change; they either go your way or they don't. It's almost as comforting to think that we might be at or near a turning point in the disease of competition for resources, the mindless over-accumulation that our economies depend upon and the exhaustion of our dowry as earth dwellers.

We need a change of mind. Not just because sea levels might rise, polar caps melt, or farmland turn to desert. We need a basic change of mind to understand what has brought all this on us. We need to see that it's time to relinquish the supposed mandate of Darwin, which has us ripping each other off and glorying in it. The crisis just beginning to appear over the horizon is just a trigger for our mental change, the catalyst that has the potential to bring about *metanoia.*

Things aren't too bad for us yet. A bit of flooding in the Somerset levels, a lack of snow in our favourite skiing destination. We can still roll over and go back to sleep for a while. But even then, we will feel a nagging sense of unease, like dogs that bark before earthquakes.

If we are as progressive as we claim, we will find a way to take note of those distant rumblings. We will not wait until the queues for bread arrive at Tesco, or the lights wink out in Newington Green. We will learn to see in the bad news, which we are newly determined to face, a glimmer of light.

That sounds a bit like a cue, doesn't it?

How Can I Love People when They're All So Wrong?

I'm trying not to watch the news these days. Every time I do, I seem to get more upset.

The awful events in my home country have been very much on my mind. Every other day, it seems, another alienated kid with a too-easily purchased gun has what he thinks of as his day in the sun. Kids and bystanders are dead and injured as a result. To make things even worse, it all happens in a political and social atmosphere that has been called "toxic" by nearly everyone. Radio chat show hosts on both sides of the political divide hurl invective at their opponents that makes the silly insult-trading of Parliament seem tame.

Everybody else is so wrong, have you ever noticed that? If only they would learn that what I think is the only true and right way, the world would be a much happier place, wouldn't it? Well, wouldn't it? I'm sure you all agree.

I don't actually say things like that. At least I hope I don't, but it does occur to me that at my opinionated, self-righteous worst I am saying something very similar. My better self says that I should listen to the people with whom I disagree, that I should practise what I learned in counselling training about empathy. The old saying goes, "Don't condemn a man until you have walked a mile in his moccasins." That's probably why I laughed when I read a recent line on some website or other that said, "Don't condemn a man until you have walked a mile in his shoes. That way you'll be a mile away, and you'll have his shoes!"

When I worked in Botswana in the 1980s, I lived in a centre for refugees of the scourge called *apartheid.* My friends were black South Africans whose lives had been ruined by racism and oppression. Some of them had been tortured; one had come through a hole in the fence with three bullets in his body. I read Nelson Mandela and Steve Biko and talked freedom. I got mad at the Quakers I worked for because they wouldn't let ANC members stay on the centre; they were believers in armed violence, said the local meeting.

I hated white South Africans. I say that in sorrow because I was wrong. I found out just how wrong when I got back. I met a young minister of the Dutch reformed Church, a man who until three years previously, had preached the gospel of *apartheid.* Literally finding in Bible passages how God intended the blacks to be the servants of the white, superior race. He had been passionate about this, and – as he explained – he was able to hold this view because he saw blacks as objects, not people. Objects could be loaded on trucks and sent into the barren mountains. They could be forced to carry passports in their own country, even, if they got frisky, be shot in the street. All of this could be justified by the Bible.

One day Patrick got hold of a banned copy of *My Life with Martin Luther King,* by Coretta Scott King. Amused, he began to read. Here's what he told me of that moment. "Art, they were so right to ban that book. By the end of the first chapter my life was beginning to change. Not because of any greatness on the part of Martin Luther King; I couldn't see that yet. But because it suddenly occurred to me that King was a *person,* just like me." He reportedly spent days praying and weeping, and when he was done, preached an anti-apartheid sermon from his own pulpit, to who can imagine what condemnation. He was sacked, virtually defrocked and evicted from the parsonage. His family reviled him. He joined the fledgling UDF (United Democratic Front) and became a non-violent activist. Finally, he went into exile. He was one of the most remarkable people I ever met.

His appearance in my life did the same thing for me as the book had for him. I saw him not as a Boer fascist, but as a person, just like me. He made me realise that when you hate people, you don't really see them; they're just objects to be manipulated or ignored. *Depersonalised.* Like white South Africans. Like shack dwellers in Cape Town. Like Iraqi peasants. Like little specks below your stealth bomber, too tiny even to be seen.

Depersonalisation happens when we allow ourselves the dirty little secret pleasure of a racial epithet. It happens when the behaviour of someone "foreign" to us is used as an example of their inferiority, as when an Asian jumps a queue. It happens when we interpret body language and dress style as defiance of "decent" behaviour. It happens every time a train crash in Bangladesh or Bolivia that kills 700 people winds up on page 11 of the newspaper. It happens when we count the towels on the beach chairs that the Germans left or avoid three young black men on a street corner. It happens now when otherwise decent people start complaining about the influx of immigrants. Every time depersonalisation happens, a tiny seed of war is sown. Not by the US administration or the president of Iran; by us.

So the question "Where is peace to be found?" leads us – guess where? That's right, back to our very own selves. You don't have to dig very far into the lives and words of the great sages to find this. Jesus talking about "loving your enemy" and the "beam in your own eye" and "turning the other cheek." Buddha and his path of compassion. The *wu wei* of Taoism and Zen. The mercy of Allah. Satyagraha of Gandhi. Shall I keep on? Or shall I stay with the first moral question in Hebrew literature: "Am I my brother's keeper?"

War is often compared to a fire starting. First you have a little spark; nothing much, really. But there is always plenty of fuel about, nice dry sticks of racism, nationalism, prejudice and self-interest. And before you know it, the forest is ablaze, and Bambi and Thumper are running for their lives. When that happens, there is just one thing you can do: pray for rain. Pray for peace and the collective yearning might just yield its own miracle, exhaust the heat and cool the flames, and let things go back to their smouldering.

But the fire will come again and again until we start to understand that we are the authors, instigators and causes of conflict. Until we take it upon ourselves to dampen the dry fuel of hatred. Make no mistake about this: wars may be brought to fruition in staff rooms and field headquarters, but they begin here in the individual and collective mood of people. Here, not over there.

My late friend Adam Curle was a Quaker and Tibetan Buddhist. He was the founder of the Chair of Peace Studies at Bradford University. When I was involved in a conflict once, he was my combination guide and lawyer. He told me about something called "Shambala Warriors". These are people who secretly practise the art of ending war and violence. They are an old Tibetan legend, but some groups of them really exist. They understand, said Adam, that the reservoir of war is the human heart, which is also the reservoir of love. The trick is to practise "intentional loving". That is, to love someone you cannot easily love: murderers, foreigners, enemies. He said that even a small beam of love sent bravely from the heart does wonderful things. You see, he knew that hatred begets hatred, fear begets fear, punishment begets revenge. Beat a child and he will beat others. Hug him in his pain and fear and he will learn to love. That's the reason that we're all responsible. No matter how far away a war may be, it's as near as your own breast. There is no way to stop outside wars without stopping inside ones. We're all in charge of that.

That may sound easier than it is. We are used to thinking of love as something that just happens, as when you fall in love. Or when being around someone for years gradually makes the relationship loving, whatever the disagreements may be. It takes a little imagination to love someone who is unlovable. So how is it to be done?

The solution is that little word: empathy. Empathy isn't sympathy. Remember the parable of the Good Samaritan? Despite what Margaret Thatcher famously said about its proving there is "no such thing as society" it makes a good departure point. Sympathy would have made the Samaritan's heart melt with pity, but he might just have lost his effectiveness in dealing with the injured man's problem. Sympathy is often reserved, in any case, for furry animals and little children, not for wrong-doers and members of an enemy tribe. Antipathy would have left the Samaritan cold; the plight of the victim would have meant nothing to him. But empathy enabled him to imagine his way into the state of the injured man. He could envision the difficulties he was experiencing without undue emotion and be really helpful.

So maybe "intentional loving" is more about being willing to explore the position of the other, rather than waiting for floods of sympathetic tears and feeling your heart go pitty-pat. Maybe we can't feel emotion that swells in our breasts when an asylum seeker winds up afoul of our laws. But maybe we can understand it a bit and make judgements about it based on what is ultimately helpful instead of railing in self-justified anger. And when it is necessary to oppose someone's position, I need to make sure that I am opposing that – their position – and not their history, his accent or his hairstyle. Not easy, not easy at all, but I believe it is the only way through this seemingly never-ending round of slaps and kisses. It is the only way to stop new battles and clashes from beginning. When we expunge the poison of anger, we make the future possible. Make it possible in ways that now seem increasingly unlikely.

So what do you say to this? Shall we start now? Let's do what we know we must. Let's get started with the intention of loving someone that we cannot love. Maybe it will be a foreigner; maybe someone who has hurt us. Not loving in any phoney or hypocritical way. Meher Baba said, "True love is no game for the faint-hearted and weak; it is born of strength and understanding." Skirmishes come and go, but there is a larger peace to be won. And we're the folks to do it, with our little bit of love and will. Even a little drop like that, poured gladly from an exercise of intention and understanding, can do what nothing else can.

Better Angels

It's funny how small things, almost unnoticed things, have a way of becoming very important.

I have always been a keen bug-crusher. If an insect crept or flew into my personal space, I never hesitated to whack them with a newspaper or grind them under my heel. Maybe that was because I grew up in semi-tropical Florida, where bugs were literally everywhere, all year. Especially mosquitoes.

My life partner, Gilly, is different from me. I can recall seeing a big garden spider that had somehow found its way into our bath. I turned on the light and there it was, half a hand's breadth, trying to escape up the porcelain slope of the tub. My first instinct was to look around for something to smack it with. Then I heard her say, "Isn't she beautiful!" I realised that crushing the bug was not on the menu for that evening and somehow wound up manoeuvring the creature onto a sheet of paper and gently ushering it out of the window. I still didn't think its horrible little face was beautiful, but I went along with the idea. For then.

I kept on crushing bugs without feeling any different until, as I recounted earlier, one sleepy afternoon on a train a wasp, clearly declining as the days got cooler, landed on my hand. Startled, I threw it onto the floor and moved my foot to kill it, when a man sitting opposite interrupted me. He was dressed as if he had been sleeping rough; he was unshaven and shaggy-looking. 'Stop!' he said. 'Don't kill it.'

Something about his voice seemed to go right through to some core part of my nature. 'Sorry,' I said, and left the struggling creature where it was. In a few moments, it seemed to recover and flew away.

Since then, I have been a changed man. No more bug-crushing for me. No, I haven't become a Jain, wearing a face mask to prevent accidentally inhaling, and therefore destroying, gnats. I have become more sensitive to life, though and, sadly, it's begun to affect the way I view eating meat. I'll keep you informed about that. Oh, don't condemn me if I backslide

Thank God I'm an Agnostic

sometimes. I have had malaria and a life-threatening case of Dengue Fever, so mosquitoes still aren't on my conservation list.

Now I could spin you a story about how that tramp-like man on the train was an angel in disguise. I could, but I won't. What I will tell you is that he somehow woke up what Abraham Lincoln referred to as "the better angels" of my nature.

That lovely phrase may be most familiar as a part of Barack Obama's speeches. It came to him by way of Lincoln's inaugural address, given at a time of huge division in his country, which was on the brink of devastating war. Lincoln himself borrowed the phrase from Dickens, which I'll share with you a bit later. Lincoln said:

> *We are not enemies, but friends. We must not be enemies. Though passion may have strained it must not break our bonds of affection. The mystic chords of memory, stretching from every battlefield and patriot grave to every living heart and hearthstone all over this broad land, will yet swell the chorus of the Union, when again touched, as surely they will be, by the better angels of our nature.*

It will come as no surprise to you to hear that I think we are in a similar time. We are divided: in America, in Europe and here at home. It is as if something has set the wheel of our world spinning, and we have been forced, centrifugally, into opposition. As in the American civil war, families are divided, youth is in disagreement with age, races and religions are facing off, and the rhetoric most often heard is that of victory over the other side.

The noise is deafening. And we're making it even louder. It's so loud that maybe the better angels can't hear their cue. How to summon them now, when we need them the most?

Here's what Charles Dickens, sometime Unitarian, said:

> *The thoughts of worldly men are forever regulated by a moral law of gravitation, which, like the physical one, holds them down to earth. The bright glory of day, and the silent wonders of a starlit night, appeal to their minds in vain. There are no signs in the sun, or in the*

130

moon, or in the stars, for their reading. They are like some wise men, who, learning to know each planet by its Latin name, have quite forgotten such small heavenly constellations as Charity, Forbearance, Universal Love, and Mercy, although they shine by night and day so brightly that the blind may see them; and who, looking upward at the spangled sky, see nothing there but the reflection of their own great wisdom and book-learning ...

It is curious to imagine these people of the world, busy in thought, turning their eyes towards the countless spheres that shine above us, and making them reflect only the images their minds contain ... So do the shadows of our own desires stand between us and our better angels, and thus their brightness is eclipsed.

If we really want to re-acquaint ourselves with those angels, there's a clue in that passage from Barnaby Rudge. One thing that stands between us and the better angels is our own desire. Desire for things to work out the way we plan. Desire to hold onto what we imagine was a happier past. Desire to make others conform to our image, even if that means reducing them to two-dimensional figures.

Remember those cartoons we used to see as kids? An angel stands on one shoulder and a devil on the other. The devil wants us to have our own way. He has a charmingly wicked way of urging us: "Go ahead, take it." He may also speak of your entitlement: "Everything was better before those Eastern Europeans, Mexicans, Muslims, refugees came here." "Marriage is meant for one man and one woman only." "Pity about those innocent civilians, but the only way to defeat the enemy is to bomb him back to the stone age." The answers he offers are easy, logical.

Meanwhile, what the angel whispers is much less tempting. He speaks of a reality that lies beyond immediate gain and loss. He speaks to a part of you that has been buried under habit and daily detail. This part has been seduced by the slogans of the world: compete, grow rich, win. But his words don't fall on deaf ears; they fall on ears that have been deliberately ignored for the sake of safety, gain and a sense of self-righteous entitlement. Dickens and Lincoln, along with spiritual heroes of every generation since the caves, ask us to hear.

But there is even more to be learned from the angel, and as the pendulum of awareness swings, it would be a bad thing to forget it. If there is a single thing we need as a society, it is not more reductionist scientific explanations, but a renewed vision of the angelic, as Dickens says. We need to be able to look at the 14-billion-year history of the universe and still see the six days of creation. We need to see that the discovery of brain hormones like oxytocin does not invalidate love. We need to find new ways of believing old things, so that the baby doesn't escape down the plughole with the bath water. We need to look beyond the description of things to their essence. In other words, we need to be reacquainted with the holy.

As we go about explaining away everything, our angelic nature retreats further: there seems to be less and less reason to believe in the divinity within human beings. Our observations of Syrian atrocities, paedophilia and drive-by shootings confirm this. Without realising it, we are flattening the peaks and valleys of human consciousness and making the world more barren.

I don't think the better angels of our nature have disappeared. I think they are in the wings, just offstage, waiting for a cue. In times when self-interest seems to indicate the resort to violence and unfair competition, and it's tempting to let all those things your mother told you give way to selfishness, it's time to call those angels to do the work they are intended for.

I have noticed that the better angels speak softly, but often. Hearing what they have to tell us is a matter of training ourselves to listen. Otherwise, the tramp on the train is just a tramp on the train. A bug in the bathtub is not a miracle of evolution, a sacred life – just a bug in the bathtub.

Is that sunset just trapped dust particles in the air? Is the moment of death merely a flattened brain wave on the oscilloscope? And that thing your baby does with its mouth just an all-too-explainable muscular twitch which we happen to call a smile?

It's none of these, none solely of these. You know it and so do I; it's nothing less than the very face of God.

Disclaimer

Some people may wonder how a minister of a church can claim to be an agnostic. If you're one of these, I refer you to the definition in the front of the book:

Agnostic: a person who holds the view that any ultimate reality (such as God) is unknown and probably unknowable

The operant verb is "to know."

I take this to mean a conclusion reached by the mind, which has its limitations. It gives rise to creeds, doctrines and dogmas, all of which, pretty much by definition, are wide of the truth.

Please note that I didn't imply that there was not something that lies outside the narrow bandwidth of human intelligence. Something so great and all-encompassing that it can scarcely be imagined, let alone named.

I'm inspired by the words of the spiritual master Meher Baba, who said, "Seeking to understand God is like trying to see with your ears."

--Art Lester

9 781789 635478